658.022
MAR
c.1

ELMHURST PUBLIC LIBRARY

3 1135 00470 0446

S0-AFC-823

OWNING AND OPERATING A SERVICE BUSINESS

by Charles L. Martin, Ph.D.

ELMHURST PUBLIC LIBRARY
ELMHURST, IL 60126

THE
CRISP
SMALL BUSINESS &
ENTREPRENEURSHIP
SERIES

CREDITS

Editor: Kay Keppler

Layout/Design: ExecuStaff

Cover Design: Barry Littmann

Copyright ©1996 Crisp Publications

Library of Congress 95-74739
ISBN-1-56052-362-X

Limits of Liability and Disclaimer of Warranty

The author and publisher have used their best efforts in preparing this book and make no warranty
of any kind, expressed or implied, with regard to the instructions and suggestions contained herein.
This book is not intended to render legal or accounting advice. Such advice should be obtained from
competent, licensed professionals.

INTRODUCTION TO THE SERIES

This series of books is intended to inform and assist those of you who are in the beginning stages of starting a new small business venture or who are considering such an undertaking.

It is because you are confident of your abilities that you are taking this step. These books will provide additional information and support along the way.

Not every new business will succeed. The more information you have about budgeting, cash flow management, accounts receivables, marketing and employee management, the better prepared you will be for the inevitable pitfalls.

A unique feature of the Crisp Small Business & Entrepreneurship Series is the personal involvement exercises, which give you many opportunities to immediately apply the concepts presented to your own business.

In each book in the series, these exercises take the form of "Your Turn", a checklist to confirm your understanding of the concept just presented and "Ask Yourself", a series of chapter-ending questions, designed to evaluate your overall understanding or commitment.

In addition, numerous case studies are included, and each book is cross-referenced to others in the series and to other publications.

BOOKS IN THE SERIES

▶ **Avoiding Mistakes in Your Small Business**
David Karlson, Ph.D.

▶ **Budgeting for a Small Business**
Terry Dickey

▶ **Building Teams for Your Small Business**
Robert B. Maddux

▶ **Buying a Business: Tips for the First-Time Buyer**
Ronald J. McGregor

▶ **Buying Your First Franchise: The Least You Need to Know**
Rebecca Luhn, Ph.D.

▶ **Extending Credit and Collecting Cash**
Lynn Harrison

▶ **The Female Entrepreneur**
Connie Sitterly

▶ **Financial Basics of Small Business Success**
James O. Gill

▶ **Getting a Business Loan: Your Step-By-Step Guide**
Orlando J. Antonini

▶ **Great Customer Service for Your Small Business**
Richard F. Gerson

▶ **Human Relations in Small Business**
Elwood N. Chapman

▶ **A Legal Guide for Small Business**
Charles P. Lickson

▶ **Managing the Family Business: A Guide for Success**
Marshall W. Northington, Ph.D.

▶ **Marketing Strategies for Small Business Success**
Richard F. Gerson, Ph.D.

▶ **Nobody Gets Rich Working for Somebody Else**
Roger Fritz

▶ **Operating a Really Small Business**
Betty M. Bivins

▶ **Owning and Operating a Service Business**
Charles L. Martin, Ph.D.

▶ **Personnel Management for a Small Business**
Neville Tompkins

▶ **Your New Business: A Personal Plan for Success**
Charles L. Martin, Ph.D.

v

Dedication

To Marilyn; my wife; teammate, and friend— with love.

Acknowledgments

Many thanks to the countless number of business practitioners, academics, students, teammates, family, and friends who have directly or indirectly helped me bring this book to fruition. Unfortunately, an attempt to list all of them individually would lead to inevitable, yet unintentional omissions. However, I would like to offer a special thanks to all of the Club 55 members in the W. Frank Barton School of Business. Their zest for entrepreneurship has made quite an impression!

CONTENTS

PREFACE   xi

CHAPTER ONE   WELCOME TO THE
                     SERVICE SECTOR   1
The Arrival of the Service Economy 3
Service and Service Businesses 5
Driving Forces of Service Opportunity 6

CHAPTER TWO   SERVICE BUSINESSES ARE
                     DIFFERENT   13
The Challenges Facing Service Businesses 15

CHAPTER THREE   SERVICE INTANGIBILITY:
                     SEEING IS BELIEVING   21
The Evaluative Dilemma 23
Service Boundaries 23
Pricing 23
Patent Protection 24
Managing the Evidence 24
Representing the Service 26
A Concluding Thought 27

CHAPTER FOUR   SERVICE HETEROGENEITY:
                     ALL SERVICES ARE NOT
                     CREATED EQUAL   29
The Variability of Service 31
The Downside: Uncontrolled Costs and
Unrealized Expectations 31
The Upside: Customization 32
Managing Unwanted Heterogeneity 32
Managing Customer Expectations 36

CONTENTS (continued)

CHAPTER FIVE   **SERVICE PERISHABILITY: SERVICE WITHOUT INVENTORIES**   **39**

The Supply and Demand Challenge 41
Matching Supply and Demand 42

CHAPTER SIX   **SERVICE SIMULTANEITY: DANCING WITH CUSTOMERS**   **49**

The Manufacturing Contrast 51
The Challenge of Evaluating Services Prior to Purchase.........52
The Challenge of the Employee-Customer Dance.................56

CHAPTER SEVEN   **SERVICE COMPETITION: OBSCURED, EVERCHANGING, AND UNPREDICTABLE**   **61**

The Dynamics of Competition 63

CHAPTER EIGHT   **ORGANIZING THE SERVICE BUSINESS**   **71**

Evaluate Organizational Issues...73
The Organizational Service Challenge 73
The Service System 75
Design and Structure 80

CHAPTER NINE   **UNDERSTANDING SERVICE QUALITY**   **91**

Quality Doesn't Cost—It Pays 93
The Service Quality Challenge 94
What Is Service Quality? 95

CONTENTS (continued)

CHAPTER TEN   MANAGING SERVICE QUALITY   103

Measuring and Monitoring Service Quality 105

Problem Diagnosis: Using the Data 111

Finalizing the Service Quality Action Plan 114

CHAPTER ELEVEN   PERSONNEL POWER   119

The Service Personnel Challenge 121

Recruiting the Best 121

Screening the Applicants 124

Orientation of New Hires 126

Training and Development 127

Employee Coaching and Supervision 129

Employee Motivation 130

CHAPTER TWELVE   PRICING SERVICES   135

The Service Pricing Challenge 137

Costs 137

Market Demand 139

Competition 140

Objectives 141

Systems Prices 142

Nonmonetary Prices 142

Customer Beliefs and Expectations 144

Pricing Communications 146

CONTENTS (continued)

CHAPTER THIRTEEN **GROWING THE SERVICE BUSINESS** — **149**

The Service Growth Challenge 151

Benefits and Risks of Growth 152

Growth Alternatives 156

CHAPTER 14 **MANAGING CUSTOMER RELATIONSHIPS** — **171**

The Service Relationship Challenge 173

Finding the Right Mix 175

CHAPTER 15 **SERVICE LEADERSHIP: PUTTING IT ALL TOGETHER** — **193**

What is Leadership? 195

ABOUT THE AUTHOR — **203**

PREFACE

The service business is the fastest-growing sector of our economy. Since more than half of the typical household budget is spent on services, entrepreneurs correctly perceive that tapping into the service sector presents business opportunities.

However, owning and operating a service business is not the same as operating other types of businesses. The entrepreneurial challenges and business emphases differ. This book diagnoses dozens of such challenges and suggests how to overcome them. For example, because services are intangible, costs can be more difficult to monitor and control. What should the owner do? *Owning and Operating a Service Business* can help.

This book is not a substitute for books that explain the ins and outs of starting a new business, nor should it replace books that discuss specific areas of business such as management, marketing, finance, human resource management and accounting. Rather, this book picks up where the others leave off—by highlighting the entrepreneurial and business issues you will face in the service sector.

CHAPTER
ONE

WELCOME TO THE SERVICE SECTOR

CHAPTER ONE

THE ARRIVAL OF THE SERVICE ECONOMY

Welcome to the service sector of the 1990s—the portion of our economy (now the largest part) that is characterized by the sale of intangibles and driven by ideas, information and people helping people. As the relative size of the manufacturing sector has declined over the past several decades, the service sector has come to dominate the U.S. economy. In a sense, every business today is a service business, because every business is in the business of serving its customers. Today, service is the business of business.

People used to buy goods. For more than 350 years, when people plunked their money down, they bought land or mules or saws; they bought plows or gunpowder or seeds; they bought cloth or flour or books or homes or cars. Then in 1985, for the first time in U.S. history, consumers spent more for services than for things. Today, about 54% of the typical family's budget is spent on services, which include a wide range of purchases.

Revenues in the service sector have grown since the mid-1980s at almost twice the rate of other industries. Since 1980, the annual rate of employment growth in the service sector has been about three times that of other industries. During the same period, the service sector has accounted for more than two-thirds of all new jobs in the United States, and that proportion is expected to increase in the years ahead.

Not surprisingly, service businesses are well represented among the hottest entrepreneurial opportunities of the 1990s. In fact, one expert's Top Ten list for the 1990s includes nothing but service businesses*:

1. Catering

2. Computer and office machine repair

3. Day care

4. Educational services and products

5. Career counseling

---

*Gumpert, David (1991), Ten Hot Businesses to Start In the 1990s, *Working Woman*, 16 (June), 55–56+.

6. Financial planning

7. Home health care

8. Printing, copying, and mailing

9. Marketing, promotion, and public relations

10. Senior fitness and recreation

Selected Service Industries in the United States: Annual Receipts (in billions of dollars)				
Type of Service Business	1985	1989	1992	Percent Increase 1985–1992
Hotels, other lodging	45.4	59.0	64.0	42.3
Personal services (laundry, beauty shops, portrait studios, etc.)	36.7	52.1	59.1	61.0
Business services (advertising, employment agencies, data processing, etc.)	155.9	249.1	302.6	94.1
Automotive services (repair, rental)	51.7	71.7	79.5	53.8
Misc. repair services	20.7	30.3	36.3	75.4
Motion pictures	21.6	35.0	43.8	102.8
Amusement, recreation services	31.2	42.2	51.1	63.8
Health services	147.4	220.1	285.0	93.4
Legal services	52.8	81.4	96.2	82.2
Engineering/architectural services	49.3	70.0	75.8	53.8
Accounting, auditing, bookkeeping	21.2	32.2	37.0	74.5

Source: Statistical Abstract of the United States, 1994.

Moreover, many service industries grow even during economic downturns. For example, the U.S. economy was suffering the effects of a recession in August 1992. During that month, U.S. manufacturers cut 97,000 jobs, while retailers and construction businesses trimmed their payrolls by 71,000 and 7,000 jobs, respectively. Mining jobs declined for the 18th consecutive month, but service industry jobs increased by 20,000.*

Still, service entrepreneurship is not an arena to be entered haphazardly. The management skills, business priorities and entrepreneurial style that may create success in other industries do not necessarily translate into service success. Service businesses present different issues, emphases and challenges that create a different entrepreneurial and managerial experience than that posed by other ventures. Before delving into those differences, however, let's examine what is meant by a service business and identify the trends that contribute to the opportunities and challenges in the service sector.

SERVICE AND SERVICE BUSINESSES

The word "service" can mean different things to different people, but from a business point of view, service means one of three things. First, service often refers to something of value that is bought and sold, but is intangible. Life insurance, consulting and airline travel are good examples. When we think of these services, we think of tangible items: contracts (insurance policy), reports (consulting) and airplanes (airline travel), but the services themselves and their accompanying value are intangible. These services, per se, cannot be seen, touched or tasted, so customers may not fully perceive the service's value. Therefore, a service business is one whose core offerings to its customers are primarily intangible.

Service also may refer to an augmented feature of a tangible product, such as the financing, delivery, installation and repair of a home appliance. Here, the business's core

---

*Rankin, Robert A. (1992), Job Loss Rekindles Fears of Recession, *Wichita Eagle*, September 5, pp. 1A+.

component is a tangible product, but the product support may differentiate one manufacturer's goods from another's and therefore create a competitive edge in the marketplace. Automobile dealerships, for example, have found that the profit potential of auto financing and repair services far outweighs the profit associated with the base sale of vehicles.

Last, service refers to how a transaction is handled. A bank may offer a competitive interest-bearing checking account and a restaurant may serve the tastiest food in town, but consumers will complain about poor service if bank tellers are not courteous and waiters are not prompt. Monitoring and controlling the quality of customer relations is very different from controlling manufacturing specifications. Thus, virtually every business may be considered a service business, and those that acknowledge their service side are more likely to succeed.

All three definitions of service will be used in this book, but since the service challenges are greatest for those businesses whose core offerings are intangible, the focus will be on these industries. Therefore, entrepreneurs, managers and marketers of businesses that primarily sell intangibles should benefit the most from this book, but manufacturers, retail store operators and administrators in other types of organizations also should be able to use some of these ideas.

DRIVING FORCES OF SERVICE OPPORTUNITY

Examining the trends and other factors that have contributed to the rise of the service sector helps us to understand how it will grow in the future. The factors of change can predict an evolving marketplace that affects customers, competitors and ultimately the business itself. Let's look at a few of these factors that are driving today's booming service sector.

Demographic Factors

Slowing Population Growth. U.S. population growth for the 1990s is expected to be only 7%, in contrast to 9.8%

in the 1980s. With a smaller pool of potential customers, competition will intensify and businesses will find that it is more cost efficient to invest resources in keeping customers than in attracting new ones. Good service, of course, plays a crucial role in retaining customers.

A slower population growth also means a shrinking pool of prospective employees. Service businesses that relied heavily on younger employees to fill service jobs in past decades are looking to older Americans to fill vacancies. Today, efforts to recruit qualified workers often resemble slick marketing campaigns that go far beyond placing ads in the classified section of the local newspaper. To stay with the company and be productive once hired, today's service workers must find their jobs interesting, their work environment pleasant and their supervisors friendly.

Some communities are not affected by slower population growth rates as much as others. Large western and southern cities, especially those located along the coasts, are the fastest-growing areas. Eight of the nation's 12 fastest-growing communities are located in Florida. Of course, business opportunities—including opportunities for service entrepreneurs—accompany this growth.

Aging of America. Lower birth rates combined with increased life expectancy rates mean that the typical U.S. citizen is about four years older today than in 1980. This trend is expected to continue as almost twice as many people reach their 65th birthday each day as those who reach their 18th birthday. This is good news for service providers of health care, retirement homes and recreational vehicles, but all service businesses can benefit by recognizing the characteristics and needs of older customers. Seniors appreciate lower prices, excellent service, fewer stairs to climb and more places to sit, larger print and less glare.

Shrinking Households. Households are getting smaller—down from 3.1 members in 1970 to about 2.5 today. More than one-fourth of today's households are occupied by only one person, and about 30% of all families are headed by a single parent. Smaller households mean fewer people to share housekeeping and other domestic chores, so opportunities abound for service entrepreneurs who help consumers save time (by housecleaning, babysitting or home delivery, etc.). Smaller households also present entrepreneurial opportunities for entertainment, recreation and leisure-time services.

Cultural Diversity.   During the 1980s, the white population grew by only six percent, compared to that of African-Americans (13%), Native Americans (38%), Hispanics (53%) and Asian-Americans (108%). This diversity trend is expected to continue for several more years. As it does, service businesses can grow by appealing to more diverse groups of customers, hiring workers that proportionately correspond to the diversity of the customer base and recognizing—even embracing—the cultural differences between groups.

Shifting Income.   Historically, most of the nation's wealth has been distributed to the middle class, with both the rich and the poor representing only a small percentage of the population. Today, a much greater proportion of individuals occupy the high and low ends.

Affluence creates opportunities for service entrepreneurs who can provide luxury or nonessential services and convenience-related services that enable wealthy consumers to trade dollars for time. Service opportunities are created at the lower end as well, usually in the form of jobs.

Rising Education Levels.   From the beginning of the century until 1960, American colleges and universities granted a total of about six million degrees. Since 1989 American colleges and universities have awarded the same number of degrees in one-tenth the time! Accompanying these rising education levels is a heightened level of expectation. Consumers expect value, and they gravitate toward service providers that meet their demands. Service entrepreneurs who expect to thrive are those who meet the service challenges posed by consumers' rising education levels.

Technological Factors

Sweeping changes in technology create new service opportunities. For example, complex electronics in automobiles and home appliances prompt the typical consumer to seek out service technicians to repair malfunctioning possessions. Past generations of consumers felt more confident in their ability to provide this sort of service for themselves.

As computers become more commonplace, service businesses can efficiently collect and analyze data about their customers, competitors, suppliers, employees and operations. This data can enable entrepreneurs to provide quicker, more accurate and more cost-efficient service.

As technology performs more and more routine tasks, employees can be released to do more complex work, including customer service. Knowledgeable, courteous and helpful service workers will become more valuable to employers as they take on a proportionately greater share of representing the company to consumers.

Political/Legal Factors

Regulation and deregulation of telecommunications, air transportation and banking have changed the way businesses compete. The resulting range of services has given consumers more options from which to choose.

Lack of Time

Many people today lack time. The work week is longer by 2.5 hours than it was in 1970. Commutes are longer. In most two-parent households, both parents work. The challenge and the opportunity for entrepreneurs is to free consumers' time. Do this first by having a service that emphasizes convenience, and then make it the best service available.

Competitive Manufacturing

As manufacturers become more competitive, they use services to enhance the attractiveness of their goods. For example, more than 10,000 manufacturers of products found in grocery and drug stores have added toll-free product support hotlines since 1967. Manufacturers of consumer durables and industrial products also may deliver and install products free of charge, teach customers how to use them, guarantee them or arrange attractive financing.

Hollowing of Organizations

More businesses are contracting out services they once performed themselves—such as janitorial, legal, accounting, telemarketing and marketing research services—to lower costs. If you are an entrepreneur interested in serving business customers rather than consumers, you might begin by examining industries that are familiar to you. Break down all the industry's functions and jobs into component parts. Then consider which of these pieces you could perform better or cheaper than the businesses you intend to serve.

SUMMARY

The service sector has become a dominant force in the U.S. economy. Since services now account for more than half of all household purchases, entrepreneurs have ample opportunities to succeed. The emergence of these opportunities is fueled by demographic, social, technological and other trends.

Despite the widespread opportunity for service entrepreneurship, owning and operating a service business is not quite the same as owning and operating other kinds of businesses. However, to some extent, every business is a service business.

ASK YOURSELF

► How much of your household budget goes to services?

► Recall the last major appliance or auto you purchased. What role did service play in your choice? That is, was service an important consideration?

► List several new service businesses that now exist in your community that did not exist five years ago. What are the underlying trends that have given birth to these businesses?

CHAPTER
TWO

SERVICE
BUSINESSES
ARE
DIFFERENT

THE CHALLENGES FACING SERVICE BUSINESSES

Regardless of the growth of the service sector and the factors that cause it, an entire book about owning and operating a service business would hardly be justified unless there were some uniquenesses that indicate a different entrepreneurial or managerial approach. Of course, every industry—service or otherwise—has some idiosyncracies and traditions that make it at least a little different. Working within the industry or otherwise being familiar with it before starting your own business is always a good idea, even if you decide to break away from some of the industry's norms and trappings.

Setting aside these industry-specific differences, however, several broader issues pose distinctive challenges for service businesses. Specifically, services are intangible, heterogeneous, perishable and simultaneously produced and consumed. Also of consideration are the competition in the service sector and the service business's relationship with its customers.

Intangibility

A service itself cannot be seen, touched or tasted. It is intangible. Because it is intangible, customers may not clearly understand the service or its value, and employees may not understand what the service is. Because the service may leave no visual impression, customers may not remember it, employees may find it difficult to deliver, supervisors may not be able to explain it, quality inspectors may find little to inspect, the company's attorney may have nothing to patent, accountants may not know what to cost, salespeople may find it difficult to demonstrate and the advertising agency may find it difficult to display.

Service businesses can strive to make the service itself or the company image more tangible. Many service businesses offer giveaways to their customers, develop identifiable logos, maintain the decor and cleanliness of their office and equipment and enforce dress, grooming and conduct codes for customer-contact employees.

Heterogeneity

Services tend to be heterogeneous, meaning that one unit of service is likely to vary from the next. Indeed, services may vary from business to business, location to location, employee to employee and from minute to minute. When service varies too much, costs become difficult to control. More seriously, excessive variation means customers don't know what to expect from one purchase to the next. When expectations are not grounded, customers are likely to be disappointed with the service.

Services that are labor intensive, in particular, tend to be heterogeneous because human beings cannot produce services with the same precision that machines can produce goods. Quality control in the manufacturing sector involves product specification and control, but the specification and control of human behaviors is subjective, difficult to measure and not easily controlled. However, if service heterogeneity can be planned and controlled, the service may be customized to meet the requirements of individual customers.

Perishability

Services are highly perishable in that they cannot be stored or inventoried. When a commercial airliner takes off with empty seats, that revenue is lost forever. The empty seats on that flight cannot be saved until needed. The extra seats perish. Conversely, if the plane is filled and prospective passengers are left at the gate, potential revenue again goes unrealized. The service opportunity perishes when the plane leaves the runway.

Manufacturers can build inventories during periods of low demand and deplete them during periods of high demand. However, to operate at optimum levels of efficiency, service businesses must manage the timing of supply and demand so that as many customers are served as possible with as little excess as possible.

Simultaneity

Services are simultaneously produced and consumed. An airline passenger receives air transportation as the plane is in flight, a barber's customer receives a haircut as the barber works and an attorney's client receives advice as the attorney speaks. This means that service customers may have little, if any, opportunity to evaluate their choice before purchase. Most of the evaluation may take place after the service is received, at which point the customer already may be dissatisfied and the service irreversible.

Simultaneity suggests that employees and customers will encounter one another in the process of specifying and producing the service. Patients and physicians will interact to diagnose an illness. Fast food restaurant employees interact with customers to take their orders. These employee-customer encounters are difficult to standardize and supervise, yet the behaviors of front-line employees are critical in customers' perception of the service. Contact with unprofessional or poorly trained employees may leave customers disenchanted with the service.

Competition

Competitors in the service sector are not always easily identifiable, and the mix of competitors changes constantly. Service businesses may compete against other service businesses in the same or related industry (bank vs. savings and loan), in different industries (movie theater vs. mini-golf course), against manufacturers (appliance repair shop vs. manufacturer of low-cost disposable appliances) or prospective customers (an auto oil change center vs. a do-it-yourselfer).

Because the costs of starting service businesses are often relatively low, competitors may enter the marketplace literally overnight, and they may exit just as quickly. However, the ease of starting a service business can attract unqualified providers who lack the training, experience and commitment needed to be successful. Their lack of qualifications may leave a string of dissatisfied customers in their wake and tarnish the image of the entire industry.

Relationships

The quality of the relationships between a service business and its customers often defines the service business's success. Strong relationships mean repeat patronage, and repeat patronage leverages profits. Of course, it is advisable for any business to cement relationships with its customers, but the importance is magnified in most service businesses because of customer-employee interactions, the difficulty of evaluating service quality before purchase, the affect of word-of-mouth advertising, and the almost inevitable likelihood that errors will occur, which are more likely to be forgiven if customers are convinced that the business cares. Ultimately, customer relationships can be as valuable to a service business as its staff or physical assets.

Your Turn

Conduct informational interviews with service business operators in the community. Ask them what they like and don't like about operating their businesses, what their greatest challenges are, what they do to cope with the unique characteristics of services. The information may help you decide which service industry to enter and how to plan for the business's success.

ASK YOURSELF

▶ Have you ever felt uneasy about buying a service because you were not sure exactly what you were getting?

▶ Have you ever been frustrated by a service business because the quality of the service was not as high as it had previously been?

▶ How many service businesses are located in your neighborhood? How many were not there one year ago?

CHAPTER
THREE

SERVICE INTANGIBILITY: SEEING IS BELIEVING

CHAPTER THREE

THE EVALUATIVE DILEMMA

The most commonly cited distinction of service businesses is the intangibility of what they sell. Airline passengers don't buy the airplane; they buy the transportation from one city to another. Taxpayers don't buy an accountant; they buy the time and skills the accountant uses to perform the tax work.

The intangibility factor creates a dilemma for customers and service businesses. Customers find it difficult to evaluate something that is intangible. Service workers may find it difficult to demonstrate the service in memorable ways. The value of the service may not be apparent, and service quality may be recognized only when it is absent. Banking customers may have little appreciation of the work involved in processing a check, so they might object to paying service fees on checking accounts.

SERVICE BOUNDARIES

Intangibility makes the transaction between business and customer vague. It is not always clear what one is buying and where the responsibility of the service business ends. A homeowner might hire a contractor to reroof the house, but the homeowner and contractor might disagree about cleanup or the extent to which shrubs and gutters will be protected from roofing debris. Not surprisingly, consumer complaints to the Better Business Bureau about services outnumber those about tangible goods, and service-related complaints are the least likely to be satisfactorily resolved. Therefore, it is advisable to learn what customers' expectations are and then explain or negotiate what the service does.

PRICING

The labor and materials used to produce services are usually less tangible than those used to produce manufactured items, so determining how much it costs to make a unit of service is often imprecise. Because the business's costs are a key pricing ingredient, the process of establishing prices becomes imprecise as well.

Because the service may not be understood, customers may object to prices they consider inflated. However, customers consciously or unconsciously use price as an indicator of quality. If the price is too low, prospective customers may assume the service is of inferior quality or that the service provider is taking shortcuts.

PATENT PROTECTION

With rare exceptions, only tangible items—not services—can be patented. This means that service innovations can be stolen by competitors, so it is difficult to maintain a long-term competitive advantage by offering unique services. Service entrepreneurs do have some innovation protection: They may be able to patent the specially developed equipment used to produce the service, they can obtain trademark protection for the service's unique name and logo and they can copyright literature and software.

MANAGING THE EVIDENCE

No service business can completely counter issues that intangibility presents, but a few strategies can help. One approach is to manage the evidence. Recognize that although the service itself is intangible, other elements of the business are not. The decor, appearance and demeanor of employees, the image conveyed by the company logo and letterheads, signage, location of the service facility, promotional materials and prices also send signals.

Because it is difficult to judge the intangible service, customers use tangible evidence to form impressions about the quality of service. The tangible evidence also signals the business's commitment to detail, the professionalism of employees, the attitude of management and the up-to-dateness of the service operation. Examples: Hospital patients may form a negative impression of the hospital if they see dirty rooms, dead plants in the hallways and blood-stained staff uniforms. Investors may doubt the competence of their stock broker if sales letters contain misspelled words or typographical errors.

Managing tangible evidence does not always mean extreme efforts to upgrade or modernize facilities or dress up employees. Although facility facelifts and a professional employee look are often justified, if the decor is too lavish customers may infer that management is wasteful or that prices are too high. If personnel are too well-dressed, customers may feel underdressed or perceive the atmosphere to be too formal when a relaxing atmosphere is desired. Knowing what customers consider appropriate will help you to avoid mistakes when managing the evidence.

Sign, Sign, Everywhere a Sign . . .

Every tangible aspect of the business that customers encounter may leave a lasting impression—and the impression may not be a positive one. Consider the negative impressions that these signs might make, all of which were found displayed in full view of customers.

- Restaurant in Carlsbad, New Mexico:
  Absolutely no student checks

- Auto body shop in Wichita, Kansas:
  Our credit manager is Helen Waite. If you want credit, please go to Helen Waite.

- Gift shop in Atlanta, Georgia:
  If you break it, you buy it

- Restaurant in Jacksonville, Florida:
  Never argue with a fool . . . people might not know the difference

- Convenience store in Anza, California:
  No two party checks accepted! No acceptions (sic). Don't even ask!

- Motel in Ocala, Florida:
  Suggestions welcome. They're good for a lot of laughs.

- Bowling center near Poughkeepsie, New York:
  Everyone here brings happiness—some by coming in, others by leaving

---

REPRESENTING THE SERVICE

Try to make your service more tangible. The more tangible you can make your business, the more your customers will remember you. For example:

- ▶ An automobile garage might give customers complimentary key chains with the garage's name, address and phone number

- ▶ An accountant might give clients a booklet of helpful tax tips

- ▶ A consultant might submit a professionally prepared report at the conclusion of the assignment

- ▶ An appliance service technician might return broken, replaced parts to customers

- ▶ A video rental store might give customers catalogues or brochures that describe featured rental movies of the month

- ▶ A hotel might provide soap, matchbooks or maps that display the hotel's name and logo

- ▶ A tour guide might give tourists a commemorative picture album

- ▶ A zoo or museum might open a gift shop

In all of these above examples, the concept is the same—customers receive something tangible to remind them of the service or to enhance their perceptions of the service's value. But it is not always necessary to put something tangible in the customer's hand to make the service seem more tangible. Images and pictures can help to make the service easier to understand and remember. Insurance and financial conglomerates do a great job of this. For example, All-State's good hands and Traveler's umbrella represent security benefits. Prudential's rock represents the company's stability and Merrill Lynch's bull symbolizes strength. These symbols help to sell an organizational image, which paves the way for marketing employees to sell financial products.

A CONCLUDING THOUGHT

Efforts to manage the evidence and represent the service are more important for some service businesses than for others because some services are inherently more intangible, and therefore more abstract than others. In one study*, consumers were asked to rank the tangibility of various services. Eye exams, golf lessons, city bus rides, teeth cleaning and dance lessons were rated near the intangible end of the continuum, but consumers perceived bicycles, cameras, vacuums and VCRs to be almost entirely tangible. Restaurants, furniture rental stores and auto muffler shops were rated nearer the middle of the continuum. So, the more intangible the service, the greater the need to attend to the physical cues of the business and to make the service more tangible.

---

*Hartman, David E., and John H. Lindgren, Jr. (1993), Consumer Evaluations of Goods and Services, *Journal of Services Marketing*, 7(2), pp. 4–15.

ASK YOURSELF

► Think about the last service business you visited. What physical cues in the business signaled something to you about the quality of the service or the competence of the employees? What cues in the business might have been changed to improve your perceptions?

► All of a company's products are partially tangible and partially intangible. In what ways are the following products both: car wash, auditing, advertising, fast food, education?

► How will you represent your service to make it appealing to prospective customers?

CHAPTER
FOUR

SERVICE HETEROGENEITY: ALL SERVICES ARE NOT CREATED EQUAL

THE VARI-ABILITY OF SERVICE

Not every unit of service will be delivered in the same way. This variability is called heterogeneity, and services are more heterogeneous than manufactured goods. For example, consumers will know what to expect each time they open a box of breakfast cereal, but the dining experience at a restaurant may never be repeated. Of course, the service may vary from one restaurant business to the next, but it also may vary from one location to another in the same chain, from one server or cook to another at the same location, and even from hour to hour for the same staff.

The phenomenon is not always a bad thing. Service heterogeneity can also help a business.

THE DOWNSIDE: UNCONTROLLED COSTS AND UNREALIZED EXPECTATIONS

Sometimes service variability is random or uncontrolled. Employees may spend different amounts of time and materials providing the service, which makes it difficult to control costs and set prices. Inferior quality service may have to be redone, further driving up costs.

For customers, random variation in service may be stressful if they never know what level of service quality to expect. For example, even when trips go smoothly and the service is excellent, a traveler still might worry whether the airline will arrive on time, whether the luggage will be lost or whether the hotel will honor the reservation.

In other instances, customers may expect a certain quality of service stemming from the business's advertised promises, or customers may base their expectations on past experiences with the service provider or competitors in the industry. If these expectations are not met, customers may place demands on the service business to rectify the situation, stop patronizing the business or tell others about the broken promises and poor service.

THE UPSIDE: CUSTOMIZATION

A consumer who opens a box of breakfast cereal may know precisely what to expect from the product, but if the cereal is too sweet, the customer has to change brands. It is impractical for the cereal manufacturer to customize each box of cereal to the exacting specifications of millions of customers.

It is not always so impractical for a service business to respond to customers' individual tastes and extend service beyond normal boundaries. A restaurant may prepare a less sugary breakfast upon request. An airline may be able to accommodate a tall passenger's need for a seat with extra leg room. A bank teller may be able to verify a customer's account balance before the official monthly statement is prepared. An attorney can craft legal documents to honor a client's wishes. Many services can customize their business—thereby giving customers more value and earning their loyalty.

Some businesses can inexpensively let customers perform some of the service tasks themselves. The popularity of self-service salad bars attests to the viability of such a strategy. In some service settings, however, customers may resist self-service. They may not have the skills, time or interest to perform the service for themselves, so it is advisable to offer a full-service option or have employees available to assist customers.

MANAGING UNWANTED HETEROGENEITY

Managing service heterogeneity begins with understanding what causes it. Perhaps the most important element is understanding people. Most service industries are very labor intensive, and human workers are prone to variation in how they perform. Employees bring different levels of skill, motivation and biases to the workplace. Unlike machines, service workers get tired, hungry and bored, and they can be distracted. Inevitably they make mistakes.

Knowing that service workers are not machines, management should avoid treating them as if they were. Employees should have multiple tasks to avoid boredom and sufficient break periods. Training, service standards, automation, improved systems and control of input variability also help to eliminate unwanted service heterogeneity. Avoiding the temptation to overpromise, developing a service recovery plan and strengthening relationships with customers also will help to minimize the undesirable consequences of service heterogeneity. Let's examine these prescriptions more closely.

Training

Training helps workers to be more consistent. In many service businesses, it is difficult to monitor employees' performance once they start work. Therefore, training should be as thorough as practical before employees begin their duties. It is not the customer's job to train employees, nor should customers suffer the consequences of substandard service from a poorly trained employee. If employees will serve customers, training should include a personal dimension (smiling, establishing rapport, handling irate customers), as well as a technical one (order processing, operating cash register). Follow-up, on-the-job training and coaching can be used to reinforce earlier training lessons.

Guidelines and Standards

As important as training is, however, it is not enough. Rules-of-thumb or service specifications must accompany the training. Rules-of-thumb are most appropriate when employees need flexibility in resolving problems. Some service firms empower employees to address any customer complaint that can be settled for less than a specified amount, such as $25. Others instruct employees to honor all customer requests unless employees obtain their supervisors' permission not to honor them.

When employees have less need for flexibility and all employee tasks can be identified, then exacting service standards may be developed. McDonald's Ray Kroc developed specific service standards in the 1950s before the rest of the industry realized the importance of reducing the random variation in food and service quality. Today, the operations manual for McDonald's restaurants is more than 600 pages long. It specifies every task—the amount of condiments placed on each burger, for example, and the order in which they should be put on the bun.

Automation

Automating service functions otherwise performed by employees is another strategy for minimizing human errors. Some degree of automation is available in almost every service industry—from automatic teller machines (ATMs) that replace human bank tellers to automatic pinspotters and scorers that replace pin boys and scorekeepers in bowling centers. McDonald's has tested griddles that simultaneously fry both sides of hamburger patties. Doing so removes the flipping variability of human cooks.

In some instances the automation can minimize errors without eliminating the human role. Financial brokers can get very busy handling trades for investors, and sometimes during rush periods brokers only partially process the paperwork for trades they intend to execute a few minutes later. As time passes, brokers can forget important details about the postponed transactions. Computer software can lock the screen until all the necessary information is entered. By not allowing brokers to skip to the next transaction before completing the previous one, automation helps to reduce human mistakes.

Systems

Many mistakes are understandable and not the workers' fault. Often the design of the service system is to blame. The details involved in delivering most services are so numerous that they can be performed accurately and promptly 100% of the time only by superhumans. A major hotel chain, for example, reports 152 service steps involved in preparing a guest's room. When these steps are multiplied by hundreds of guests daily, occasional mishaps will happen. Although dozens of steps may be involved in the smooth delivery of the service, it takes only one omission on one step (such as a misplaced reservation) for the entire service to collapse. This situation is more likely to occur in assembly-line service systems, in which one employee is responsible for only one step of a multistep process.

Input Variability

Employees' requirements for the job (input)—including supplies, ingredients, tools and equipment, the nature of the service task, even the customers served—and their variation will affect workers' ability to provide a consistent level of service. Employees may have little or no control over these inputs. An appliance repair technician might be expected to diagnose as many brands of toasters with just as many types of malfunctions in a month as a manufacturing worker might encounter in a lifetime. Needed parts may not be available, or toasters may be beyond repair. A computer technician answering calls on a 1-800 service line may have to help a spectrum of customers whose disposition, tolerance for frustration, communication skills and computer literacy vary.

Reducing input variability may involve working more closely with suppliers to ensure desired consistency of materials and supplies or it could mean refocusing the service business (limiting repair to certain brands). More seasoned employees can be assigned more difficult tasks or more challenging customers.

MANAGING CUSTOMER EXPECTATIONS

Eliminating unwanted variation in service quality is a good goal, but some mistakes still are likely to occur. Recognizing this inevitability, try a couple of additional strategies. Don't promise customers more than the business can deliver. When expectations are not met, customers will be unhappy. You might lose some business due to unhappy customers, but employee morale and productivity may suffer as well when angry customers vent their dissatisfaction on employees.

Service Recovery

Developing a service recovery plan is a good idea. What will you do when service errors occur and the customer is wronged or inconvenienced? Consider a sincere apology, refund or compensation for the customer's loss. Ideally, several options should be available from which the dissatisfied customer can choose.

Building Bridges

Developing and maintaining strong relationships with customers will help to smooth over most problems. Customers will tolerate occasional errors if they feel the business and its employees are sincerely committed to remedying the problem. Customers also can become more dissatisfied by the way a minor complaint is mishandled than the initial problem itself. Common ways to mishandle complaints are to make it inconvenient for dissatisfied customers to complain, challenge the legitimacy of the complaint ("In the thirteen years I've been in business, you are the first customer to complain about that!") or delay taking action. ("I can't refund your money . . . I'll have to ask the manager next week.")

SUMMARY

Largely because service businesses are labor intensive, services tend to be heterogeneous; they vary from business to business, from employee to employee and from minute to minute. Such variation can affect costs and customer satisfaction. By controlling the variability and customizing the service, entrepreneurs gain a tremendous opportunity to achieve a strategic competitive advantage.

Random, unwanted service heterogeneity may be minimized by recognizing that service workers are not machines, committing to extensive employee training efforts, establishing service guidelines and specifying standards, replacing human labor with automation, evaluating the service system, and controlling the variability of service inputs. Managing customers' expectations, developing a service recovery plan and nurturing relationships with customers are three approaches to reducing the negative consequences of service heterogeneity.

ASK YOURSELF

▶ Why are you likely to be dissatisfied with heterogeneous services even when the average level of service is good?

▶ Are all services heterogeneous? Name three examples of service businesses in your community that do a good job of minimizing unwanted service variation. How do they do it? What do these exceptions have in common? Why are they exceptions?

▶ As a self-service customer, why might you resist customizing your own service? How might the business overcome your resistance?

CHAPTER FIVE

SERVICE PERISHABILITY: SERVICE WITHOUT INVENTORIES

THE SUPPLY AND DEMAND CHALLENGE

Services are perishable. As soon as they're provided, they're gone. Although the service's benefits may linger and the service may be renewed for the next period, the service itself cannot be inventoried in the company warehouse or displayed over the customer's fireplace. When a banking customer receives a monthly statement, that month's service is history. When a golfer finishes 18 holes and leaves the clubhouse, the service vanishes.

Managing supply and demand poses different challenges for service businesses than it does for manufacturers, because manufactured products can be inventoried and the inventory can be used as a buffer against supply and demand fluctuations. Manufacturers of tennis rackets can build inventories during the winter months when sales are slow. Then when sales pick up in the spring, sellers have rackets in inventory. Unless the seasonal demand is far greater than expected, thanks to the buffer inventory of rackets, production may continue throughout the year at consistent, optimum levels, and customers need never be turned away.

Excess Supply

Service businesses must cope with the absence of buffer inventories. When supply exceeds demand. When a passenger airplane lifts off with empty seats, the revenue associated with those unsold tickets is lost forever. Similarly, service opportunities perish when seats at a restaurant remain empty in the afternoon, or when service providers are unable to schedule clients during lull periods. Low demand during the winter months may create few problems for the tennis racket manufacturer, but idle capacity at the local outdoor tennis club may be a more serious concern.

In a perfect service world, service providers would be able to manufacture service and then set it on a shelf until needed. Of course, that isn't possible, but service providers still can combat the idle capacity problem in a less-than-perfect service world. Unfortunately, stockpiling inventories of service is rarely a weapon.

Excess Demand

The second perishability dilemma occurs in the opposite situation—when capacity is insufficient to meet the demand. Airlines with planes filled to capacity may have to turn away potential passengers, and accountants may not be able to prepare all of their customers' tax returns during the first two weeks of April. However, no matter what the service business, there are limits to the amount of service that can be provided in a specific time frame, because inventory cannot be stockpiled. Capacity may be expanded by adding facilities, equipment and personnel, but these options are not always feasible on short notice.

MATCHING SUPPLY AND DEMAND

Although no solution is perfect, fortunately service entrepreneurs can work to correct the imbalances between capacity and demand. A four-step process is recommended.

The first step is to identify the patterns of demand. When are the rush periods? When are the lulls? Peaks and valleys may occur daily, weekly, monthly, seasonally, or hourly. A ski resort is busier during the midafternoon than at dusk, on weekends rather than weekdays and during winter months rather than spring. Demand patterns vary for different services: The pro shop at the ski lodge is busiest in the early mornings, while late mornings may be high demand times for guests checking out, late afternoons for check-ins, evenings for restaurant traffic and late night for bar and lounge traffic.

Next, are these patterns predictable, and if so, what causes them? By understanding the patterns, it is easier to plan to meet the demand. Depending on the service business, several factors may come into play. Here are some examples.

► Complementary business activity (traffic generated by a big sale at the store next door might help your business as well)

► Cultural norms/traditions (November/December is a peak gift-buying season; long-distance telephone use is highest on Mother's Day)

- ► Economic conditions (the demand for business services often hinges on the demand for customers' goods and services)

- ► Legal deadlines/restrictions (April 15 is tax day; community curfews may exist for minors; alcoholic beverage service may be prohibited on Sundays)

- ► Pay day (gambling casinos report an increase in business early each month, immediately after gamblers receive their paychecks)

- ► Weather (auto repair shops experience high demand during fall freezes; golf courses do not)

- ► Work/school schedules (leisuretime industries prosper during evening and weekend hours)

Third, what are the tolerable limits for demand and capacity, and what are the costs and consequences of operating outside of these limits? Service quality may suffer if demand exceeds a certain level and workers may make mistakes if they are rushed or tired. There may be a maximum number of employees that can effectively occupy the work area at the same time or simultaneously use the equipment to produce the service. The size of the physical facilities may accommodate only so many customers, but goodwill may be lost if long-standing customers are turned away or exposed to poor quality rush service. Raising the capacity level to meet periods of high demand may prevent turning away customers, but the expansion may be too costly to justify if these periods are infrequent. Serving too many customers simultaneously may spread management too thin. Too few or too many customers may create a drain on cash flow. Demand beyond a certain level may be intolerable should equipment malfunction or key personnel quit or become ill. Businesses with demand that dips below a minimum level during extended lull periods may not be economical to operate profitably without layoffs and other undesirable cost-cutting measures.

Once these trade-offs are considered and tolerable boundaries identified, the challenge is to manage supply and demand within the boundaries—ideally, to match each period's demand with an equal level of supply. This involves strategies to smooth out the peaks and valleys of demand and, whenever possible, adjusting capacity accordingly. Here are some possibilities.

► Modify operating hours. If demand is too high in the afternoon, stay open later in the evenings; if too low in the morning, don't open until noon.

► Consider alternative modes of operation. Can customers order by phone, fax or mail?

► Advertise the benefits of using the service during nonpeak times (quicker service without waiting, preferential seating, easy parking). Don't imply that service is terrible during peak periods.

► Provide a price incentive to encourage customers to use the service during nonpeak times. Long distance charges are lower in the evenings and after business hours.

► Encourage reservations, steering customers into nonpeak times whenever possible. Regretfully turn away customers who fail to make a reservation and are unable to wait.

► Sell preneed services, such as funeral arrangements, that can be planned and scheduled more efficiently on a preneed basis than when the service is needed.

► Redeploy employees as demand fluctuates from service function to service function.

► Offer off-season preventive services, such as a lawnmower repair shop that offers a tune-up, oil change and blade sharpening during the winter months.

► Market to different groups of customers who may exhibit different time preferences (retirees may prefer using the service when other customers are at work).

- ► Add new services that have a high demand at times when the demand for existing services is low (restaurants can add breakfast menus for mornings and dance floors for late evenings).

- ► Automate to reduce the time it takes to serve customers (a repair service can use power tools, or a bank direct deposit).

- ► Use technology to curtail low-demand periods (ski resorts can install snow-making machines to extend the ski season).

- ► Perform some tasks in advance of peak times (establish accounts with customers during slow periods to save time processing paperwork during higher demand periods).

- ► Enable and encourage customers to perform part of the service themselves (filling out order forms, credit applications, preference questionnaires) to reduce the time employees need to serve customers.

- ► Rent extra equipment or facilities during peak times.

- ► Hire extra part-time employees or temps during peak times.

- ► Ask existing employees to work overtime during peak periods.

- ► Schedule employee vacations and free days during slow times.

- ► For customers who wait for the service, make the wait as pleasant as possible. If they must wait on the premises, acknowledge their presence, apologize for the inconvenience, provide a comfortable place for them to wait, give them something to read or do while they wait, estimate how long the wait will be, ensure that the waiting process is fair (first come, first served), and let them know what they can do to avoid waiting in the future (make a reservation, arrive early or patronize the business at a different time).

Your Turn   *The next time you find yourself waiting for service, consider how well the business manages the waiting process. Is the wait desirable, necessary, tolerable? Does someone explain how long the wait might be and what can be done to avoid waiting in the future? Note what you do while waiting. Are you bored? What do other people do? What could the business do to make the wait more tolerable? How does the wait affect your overall satisfaction of the business and your likelihood of returning?*

SUMMARY

Because services perish as they are produced, they cannot be stored or inventoried before use. Services must be produced at the moment they are needed. This service characteristic gives rise to undesirable mismatches between supply and demand. However, service providers can reduce such imbalances and minimize their effect when they do arise. Managing capacity and demand begins with planning and analysis, followed by effort to smooth demand fluctuations and shift capacity as needed.

ASK YOURSELF

► What are the likely peaks and valleys in demand for the following services: elective surgery, home maintenance, business advertising, airline travel? What factors drive these demand patterns?

► In your business, what is the ideal number of customers that you can serve daily? What can you do to manage the fluctuations in demand most effectively?

CHAPTER SIX

SERVICE SIMULTANEITY: DANCING WITH CUSTOMERS

THE MANUFAC-TURING CONTRAST

Manufactured goods are generally produced first, then purchased and then consumed. By producing goods before purchase and consumption, the manufacturer's quality control inspectors can evaluate product quality as items roll off the assembly line. They have the opportunity to fix or replace defective items before shipment.

Especially in most retail stores, customers also can inspect and evaluate items before making a purchase decision. This prepurchase evaluation may involve a visual inspection of product features such as size, style and color and may include sampling the product by trying it on (clothes), turning it on (electronic equipment) or test driving it (cars). The attributes of one brand may be judged against the attributes of competing brands sitting next to it on the store shelf. While these customer precautions don't always result in the best purchase decision, the odds of having happy customers are far greater than if customers were not allowed an opportunity to evaluate products before purchase.

Manufactured Goods: From Production to Consumption

Production

↓

Quality Control Inspection

↓

Customer Prepurchase Evaluation

↓

Purchase

↓

Consumption

↓

Postpurchase Customer Evaluation
(confirmation of expectations)

THE CHALLENGE OF EVALUATING SERVICE PRIOR TO PURCHASE

Since services are not tangible, most customers do not have the opportunity to evaluate them before purchase, or at least not as thoroughly as they would be able to evaluate manufactured goods before purchase. Services are typically purchased first (or a purchase commitment is made), then the service is produced and consumed simultaneously. A barber's customer requests a haircut before the work is done. A homeowner buys property insurance before it is needed. A business customer commissions a consulting firm to conduct a market research study before the data are gathered.

Services: Simultaneous Production and Consumption

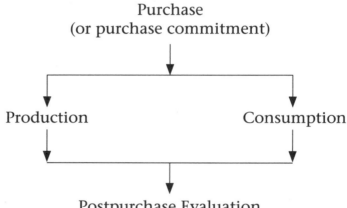

Purchase
(or purchase commitment)

Production   Consumption

Postpurchase Evaluation
(by customer and sometimes by business)

With few exceptions, service providers or customers can make adequate evaluations only after customers receive the service, if at all. Even if the service is not objectively defective, it still may not be precisely what the customers expected—possibly resulting in dissatisfied purchasers. Customers of tangible goods may be able to return or exchange purchased items if they don't meet expectations after delivery, but service customers may have nothing to return. Otherwise correcting unsatisfactory service may pose dilemmas for both the service customer and the service business. A barber's customer may be stuck with a botched haircut for a few weeks until the hair can be recut, or the timeliness of a market research study may be lost if it must be redone, and the expense of doing so may be devastating.

Business Solutions

There are several ways businesses can help customers evaluate the service and gauge their expectations before a purchase. Businesses that operate consistently, always delivering what their advertising promises, convey to customers that past experiences and the businesses' commitments are reliable indicators of future service. Such trust is critical, because customers usually do not buy services *per se*, but the promise that services will be performed.

As a service provider, you can spend extra time with new customers to learn more about their preferences and discuss what the business can do for them and what customers can expect from you. Financial planners, for example, might ask about new clients' demographics, financial status, short- and long-term goals and aversion to risk. These customer profiles are developed before specific investments are discussed. Planners have been known to turn away prospective clients that harbor unrealistic expectations.

Testimonial letters or references from previous customers, before-and-after pictures of work completed, guarantees and continuous communication with customers throughout the transaction also help to meet and shape customer expectations.

Customers' Solutions

Prospective customers also take steps to protect themselves from disappointment. These precautions include sampling and word-of-mouth communications—both of which service entrepreneurs should be familiar.

Sampling is a coping strategy often used by new customers who are not confident in their ability to evaluate the service before purchase or those who still distrust the business. When sampling, customers test the service provider by commiting to only a small amount of service and then gradually purchasing additional services or larger quantities as the business proves itself. A contractor might first be asked to renovate one room. If all goes well, the satisfied customer may then hire the contractor to renovate the rest of the building. A new banking customer might sample the bank by opening a passbook savings or checking account. Later, the customer might inquire about IRAs, credit cards, car loans and other bank services as the relationship matures.

Recognizing this strategy, astute service providers think in terms of building long-term relationships with customers, rather than in terms of one-shot transactions. This means that new accounts might appear to be only marginally profitable at first, but eventually they could be enormously profitable if the business distinguishes itself by delivering high-quality service, taking the time to communicate with customers between sales and otherwise by cultivating the relationship. To attract new customers, the business should promote low-risk, easily understood services that lend themselves to sampling. Breaking down larger quantities of service into smaller ones also facilitates sampling. For example, a health club might offer introductory one-month memberships instead of asking new customers to commit to a normal full year membership.

Customers also use word-of-mouth communication to minimize the possibility of failed expectations. Prospective customers rely heavily on the opinions and recommendations of others. Friends, family, neighbors and coworkers who have used the service are viewed as reliable and unbiased sources of information. In fact, for many services—especially professional services—word-of-mouth is the most influential source of information for new customers, so it is in the service entrepreneur's best interest to leverage word-of-mouth by increasing the number of happy customers and decreasing the number of unhappy ones.

Obviously, consistently high-quality service will create more satisfied customers who will say nice things about the business than will inconsistent or mediocre service. However, recognizing the inevitability of occasional mishaps, it is critical to encourage dissatisfied customers to vent their concerns directly to the company. Most dissatisfied service customers don't complain to the business because they don't believe the company can or will remedy the problem or because seeking redress is too time-consuming or otherwise inconvenient. Customers who don't tell you what is wrong will tell other people, often many others. In this sense, you need to increase complaints by increasing the likelihood that customers will come forward and voice their complaints when they are dissatisfied. If the business hears the complaints and remedies the problems, not only will customers be more satisfied, but they also will be more likely to spread positive word-of-mouth about how the business was concerned enough to make things right. Often it is not the original dissatisfaction that ultimately affects customers' attitudes and loyalty toward the business. Rather, what matters is how personnel respond to complaints.

Make it easy for customers to complain to you. Establish rapport with customers before they have a problem, and they will be more likely to report complaints. Give them comment cards or a telephone hotline. Empower employees to respond to customer complaints themselves. Establish a comment-reporting system so that workers can relay customer complaints to management for further analysis and action.

Quality service and extraordinary complaint-handling are not the only ways to leverage word-of-mouth. Supplying the business's most gregarious and influential customers with extra information about the company and its services encourages people to talk about your business, as do jingles, rhymes, humor, tongue-twisters and catchy slogans in advertising. Contests that involve customers in writing ad materials can be a big word-of-mouth hit. Specialty advertising items such as caps, T-shirts and coffee mugs that display the company name and logo also promote word-of-mouth and your business. Thanking and honoring loyal customers with birthday or holiday cards and awarding gifts or prizes to high-volume customers makes them feel special. Direct incentives such as gifts, discounts or cash to existing customers who refer new customers to the business can be big motivators.

The fish-bowl technique can create word-of-mouth heroes for dining, entertainment or other services used by groups of customers. Set a clear fish bowl near the cash register or other visible location, next to a sign asking customers to drop their business cards into the fish bowl for a chance to win a free meal, party, etc., for the lucky winner and a small group of coworkers or friends. For customers without business cards, slips of paper may be provided so they can participate. The technique helps the business to build a mailing list of valuable customers which, in itself, can be a tremendous marketing tool, but the benefits exceed the list. The periodic winners promote the business as they recruit new customers to enjoy the freebie. The guests usually express their appreciation by making flattering remarks about the host and the thoughtful and splendid experience, accentuating the positive aspects of the service and downplaying any negatives. If the service experience is indeed a positive one, many of the guests are likely to patronize the business in the future as paying customers.

THE CHALLENGE OF THE EMPLOYEE-CUSTOMER DANCE

To facilitate the service, workers and customers often must interact with one another. Patients discuss their symptoms with their physicians, and diners may chat with waiters about menu options and food preparation before placing their orders. If the customer's physical presence is required, as is the case for many services, the service facility and at least some of the workers may need to be located close to the customer—in the neighborhoods where customers live, work or visit. This reality often limits opportunities for rapid growth, makes economies of scale difficult to achieve and geographically spreads management thin. Beyond these issues, however, the interaction itself is highly relevant.

The employee-customer dance may vary in terms of frequency, complexity and emotional content. Some routine and automated services such as credit cards or utilities require little interaction until service is interrupted, a billing error is discovered or some other nonroutine situation arises. In some cases, the interaction may be little more than customers placing orders for a fairly standardized and well understood service, such as ordering a menu item at a restaurant. When the service is customized and more abstract, a more complex dialogue may be involved, such as when a commercial artist and a client discuss the artwork options for an ad campaign. At the extreme, customers and service providers may work together—almost as partners—to produce and consume the service simultaneously, such as when a physical therapist and patient work together in a rehabilitation effort.

Although these employee-customer interactions may sometimes appear to be simple and routine, it takes only one mishandled interaction to create a dissatisfied customer who may stop doing business with the company. Moreover, a single customer may interact with several employees at different points throughout the service experience. An airline passenger taking a single flight might encounter reservation clerks, baggage handlers, ticketing agents, gate personnel, flight attendants, pilots and other airline employees. Since each encounter could build or destroy customer loyalty, they may be thought of as moments of truth. Even smaller service businesses can have hundreds or thousands of moments of truth each day.

One of the challenges of the simultaneity phenomenon is to foster positive, relationship-building encounters between employees and customers, even though most of these encounters cannot be directly supervised or controlled. From the customer's perspective, the service employee is the service. But the technical skills of service workers may not be enough.

Employees need caring, service-oriented attitudes and sharp reasoning skills to handle each encounter effectively. Company uniforms, dress codes and other guidelines for staff appearance may be needed to convey a professional image. Communication and human relations skills also are needed.

The more complex and emotionally laden the customer encounter the greater the need for service workers to possess nontechnical people skills. Service providers must look and act like pros. They must be able to communicate effectively with customers. They must be able to establish rapport so that customers will feel relaxed and comfortable in the interaction. They must be able to restore complaining customers' confidence in the business and convert them from adversaries to allies. They must be able to ask questions skillfully to help customers articulate their preferences. They must be willing and able to listen attentively to the answers. They must be able to smile and act cheerfully and professionally, even when they are tired, bored or perturbed. And they must be able to repeat the process over and over again, from one moment of truth to the next.

In most service organizations, it is a lot to ask service workers to be all of these things, but developing personnel is part of the entrepreneurial service challenge. The failure to do so is why customers so frequently report employee behavior as a major part of their dissatisfying service experiences.

SUMMARY

Services are produced and consumed simultaneously. This service characteristic makes it difficult for the business and the customer to evaluate the service before it is sold. Hence, service businesses should strive to manage customers' expectations to avoid misunderstandings and prevent customer dissatisfaction. Providers also should seek to develop long-term relationships with customers to gain their trust and overcome the customer phenomenon of sampling. Leverage word-of-mouth advertising by encouraging dissatisfied customers to voice their complaints to the business, while encouraging happy customers to recommend the business to others.

Often simultaneous production and consumption of the service necessitates close contact between service providers and their customers. Even in a very small service business, hundreds of such encounters may transpire daily—each of which constitutes a moment of truth that can potentially build or destroy the relationship between the business and its customers. These moments of truth magnify the critical role played by front-line employees.

ASK YOURSELF

► Can you think of a service provider or business you do not trust? What happened that caused you to distrust it?

► As a service customer yourself, have you ever sampled a service before fully committing to it?

► Recall the last negative service experience you encountered. How many other people did you tell about the incident?

► How many moments of truth did you experience yesterday with service workers? How well were they handled?

CHAPTER SEVEN

SERVICE COMPETITION: OBSCURED, EVERCHANGING, AND UNPREDICTABLE

THE DYNAMICS OF COM- PETITION

Virtually every business faces some degree of competition. Service businesses are no different from manufacturers, retail stores or other businesses in this respect. What is often different for service businesses, however, is the nature of their competitors and the competitive dynamics involved. Often service competitors are not easily identified and the mix of competitors can change constantly.

Low Start-Up Costs

Service businesses are very popular among entrepreneurs. Most new businesses—and a higher percentage of entrepreneurs' first ventures—are service businesses. One reason service businesses are appealing to entrepreneurs is that service businesses have fewer entry barriers than many other types of businesses, such as manufacturing operations or retail stores. Start-up costs are generally much lower. The size of the service facility is usually smaller, sometimes requiring nothing more than a spare corner in one room of the entrepreneur's home. The equipment needed to get started may be minimal. Employees may not be needed initially. There may be no inventories to worry about, except for some supplies. On balance, it may be very viable to start small while still thinking big.

Because start-up costs often are very low, fly-by night operators might open shop nearby. They can enter the marketplace so quickly that it becomes difficult to know precisely who the competition is at any given time and how to compete against them. Because these operators might not be well trained, experienced or committed to the long-term success of their businesses, they can leave the industry as quickly as they entered it. Before leaving, however, they could slash prices in a last attempt to generate some revenue in order to recoup some of their losses. They could take shortcuts with quality and alienate customers, fail to pay their bills and otherwise develop a reputation that could tarnish the image of the entire industry. Indeed, competitors with varying degrees of qualifications and commitment who continuously come and go make for a turbulent—and therefore challenging—competitive environment.

Limited Patent Protection

Service firms cannot obtain patent protection for their services. Although the tangible equipment used to produce the service may be patented and printed material such as brochures, forms and instructional booklets may be copyrighted, there is little legal protection for services themselves. It is not uncommon for competitors to duplicate successful service concepts, making it difficult to sustain a long-term advantage in many service industries.

Shifting Costs

A tremendous range of prices can contribute to the dynamic nature of the competition as well. Some degree of price competition is found in any industry, but it can be quite intense in the service sector. Many factors help to determine price, but one of the most basic is costs. Entrepreneurs know that they must cover their costs to survive, but costs tend to be more indirect and difficult to determine in service industries than in other industries. The imprecision of determining costs can lead to under- or overpricing.

Even when costs can be determined accurately, a larger pricing problem can be traced to fixed service costs. For many service businesses, a large proportion of costs tend to be fixed rather than variable, whereas the reverse is true for manufacturers. A fixed cost is one that remains relatively constant, regardless of the volume of production. Mortgage or lease payments, property insurance, utilities and administrative salaries are examples. They change very little whether one unit is produced or if one million units are produced. Variable costs are those that vary directly with production—the greater the production volume, the higher the variable costs. Examples include supplies, materials and labor directly involved in production.

Why do high fixed costs create price instability? Although entrepreneurs recognize that they must cover both fixed and variable costs to make a profit in the long term, they also realize that only variable costs and a portion of the fixed costs need to be covered in the short term. Knowing

Cost Components for Manufacturing and Service Firms

Fixed Costs
Variable Costs

Manufacturing Costs
(high variable component)

Fixed Costs
Variable Costs

Service Costs
(high fixed component)

that fixed costs will have to be paid regardless of sales volume, entrepreneurs can be tempted to slash prices temporarily during slow periods or when faced with cash flow crises. For example, the variable costs of a hotel room may be only $7 if the room is occupied for the night, but fixed costs of $30 may be incurred regardless of whether the room is sold. To make a profit in the long term, the hotel must charge more than $37 per night ($7 plus $30), but it will lose $30 (fixed costs) if the room is not sold. So, if a group of bargain-hunting tourists wants to reserve the room during a time when it is otherwise likely to remain vacant, the hotel might sell the room for as little as $7.01. Such a deep discount would result in a long-term loss of only $29.99 instead of $30, so in this sense the hotel has experienced a short-term gain of one cent. In contrast, a manufacturer may be able to discount prices only a few percentage points before cutting into variable costs, so price fluctuations among manufacturers tend to be smaller, and therefore price competition is less intense.

Difficulty of Service Shopping

The turbulence of the marketplace could challenge prospective customers, which presents opportunities for customer-oriented service entrepreneurs. Customers may not know exactly what services a business offers compared to the competition, and they may not bother to inquire. Although several competitors might provide essentially the same service, prospective customers might be able to name only a few. Unlike shopping for tangible goods, consumers who shop for services cannot compare competing brands sitting next to one another on a retailer's shelf. They might have to call or visit each service provider individually to gather pertinent information before making a purchase decision. All of this extra work required of customers often means that they may contact only one or two service providers before an acceptable choice is found. This phenomenon has the effect of reducing the number of competitors for those businesses lucky enough to be contacted. Therefore, the individual business's challenge is to create and maintain awareness so customers will remember the company as a service option when the need for the service arises.

Once the contact is made, service providers who promptly and courteously respond have a competitive advantage. Part of the response should include answers to questions, obviously, but because the inquirer may not fully understand the service, additional information should be offered to help educate the prospective customer. Organizing and presenting this information to service shoppers in a tangible, comprehensible way will help them to develop a visual image of the service, which makes it much more memorable. Promotional brochures filled with pictures, testimonials and benefits may serve this function well.

Another useful technique to encourage favorable comparisons with competitors is called a value analysis. This tool is especially useful when there are numerous service features customers might wish to consider before making their choices, when the features might not be apparent to the untrained eye, and when trying to sort through all the options and competitors may be an overwhelming task. The chart shows an example of a value analysis worksheet provided by an apartment complex called Eaglerock Village. The apartments' desirable qualities are listed down the left side of the grid. Prospective tenants shopping for a place to live may be given a copy of the worksheet and challenged to check whether competing complexes offer the same amenities. To the extent that the service business recommending the value analysis can control the list of attributes that customers consider, they can ensure that other competitors will fail in comparison.

Example of a Value Analysis for Eaglerock Village Apartments

	Eaglerock Village	Competitor A	Competitor B	Competitor C
Microwave	X	☐	☐	☐
Heated Pool	X	☐	☐	☐
Spa	X	☐	☐	☐
Sauna	X	☐	☐	☐
Lighted Tennis Courts	X	☐	☐	☐
Recreation Room	X	☐	☐	☐
Exercise Room	X	☐	☐	☐
Three On-Site Laundry Facilities	X	☐	☐	☐
Double-Door, Frost-Free Refrigerator	X	☐	☐	☐
Dishwasher	X	☐	☐	☐
Washer/Dryer Hookups	X	☐	☐	☐
Washer/Dryer Available	X	☐	☐	☐
Woodburning Fireplaces	X	☐	☐	☐
Private Patio/Balcony with Outside Storage	X	☐	☐	☐
Assigned Night-Lighted Covered Parking	X	☐	☐	☐

Do-It-Yourselfers

Further complicating the mix of competitors in many service industries are the customers themselves. Before enlisting the professional help of a service business, customers often consider providing the service themselves. Lawn care, home maintenance, tax preparation, auto repair, transportation, child care and food preparation are a few services that do-it-yourselfers might feel confident tackling themselves. Business customers might debate whether to farm out janitorial services, advertising, marketing research, clerical services or shipping and delivery.

A study commissioned by *American Demographics* magazine discovered that do-it-yourselfers represent formidable competition in some personal service industries. Most adults (84%) do their own home decorating or ask friends or relatives to help; only 6% hire professional home decorators (10% don't decorate at all). Similarly, 85% of those surveyed who have lawns take care of them themselves or with friends and relatives; only 15% hire professional lawn care services. The study also found that only 59% of auto owners pay mechanics to repair their cars and only 51% of the taxpayers use professional accountants or tax preparation services to prepare their taxes.*

When service entrepreneurs evaluate the competitive landscape, do-it-yourselfers must be considered as one form of competition. Often this means competing even more aggressively. The success of Southwest Airlines is partially attributed to management's recognition that their chief competitors are not other airlines, but travelers who consider the advantages of flying Southwest against those of driving their cars to their destination.

Successfully competing against do-it-yourselfers means understanding why these prospective customers perform the service themselves and then building the business's service

---

*Larson, Jan (1993), Getting Professional Help, *American Demographics*, 15(July), pp. 34–38.

so that its costs and benefits will be more appealing than not. In some instances, do-it-yourselfers may believe it is less expensive to perform the service themselves, or the do-it-yourselfer option might be more convenient or result in higher quality. It might be a hobby or form of exercise, thereby creating personal satisfaction for do-it-yourselfers.

Rather than trying to counter these do-it-yourselfer perceptions directly, it may be more advantageous to build alliances with these consumers. An auto repair shop might conduct free seminars and provide instructional materials to teach community residents how to perform routine maintenance tasks and simple repairs. While seminar attendees may very well perform the routine services themselves, the rapport and goodwill established in the seminars may stimulate business for more complex auto repair work.

SUMMARY

In service competition, the mix of competitors changes continuously. Competitors can include large, well-established businesses as well as small Mom-and-Pop operations. Even customers themselves are competitors. Competitors might include first-class reputable firms, but also unprofessional and unscrupulous businesses capable of jeopardizing the reputation of the entire industry.

The cost structure of most service firms represents another competitive ingredient. Costs are largely indirect or fixed, which gives service firms considerable latitude in setting short-term prices. Inevitably such price discretion magnifies the degree of price competition, making price a potent competitive weapon.

ASK YOURSELF

► Who competes with your service business?

► What are your business's fixed and variable costs? How do they compare with those of competitors?

► Often competitors form trade or professional associations to establish service standards and train or educate industry members. Does your service industry have any such associations? What services do they provide? What are their membership requirements?

CHAPTER EIGHT

ORGANIZING THE SERVICE BUSINESS

EVALUATE ORGANI-ZATIONAL ISSUES

Service entrepreneurs neglect sometimes organizational considerations. When the business is very small, the service tasks simple and the owner works alone, the neglect may be justified. As the business grows and multiple tasks, services and employees must be managed, the value of attending to organizational issues grows.

Two sets of organizational issues are interrelated. The first issue is that of the service system.

▶ What steps will be involved in providing the service?

▶ Which steps must be performed sequentially?

▶ What sort of decisions need to be made throughout the process?

▶ What tools, equipment and supplies will be needed at each step?

▶ What will be the relative role of automation, employees and customers in providing the service?

▶ How should the layout and design of the physical environment facilitate the provision and perception of the service?

The second issue involves organizational design and structure.

▶ Who will perform each service task?

▶ What is the scope of employees' and supervisors' authority and responsibility?

▶ How much discretion do they have?

▶ Who do they report to, and who reports to them?

THE ORGANIZATIONAL SERVICE CHALLENGE

Organizational considerations are relevant to any sort of business. However, the unique characteristics of service businesses raise additional issues. For example, customers' presence in the service facility, their participation in service delivery and their interaction with employees challenge service businesses.

If the customer's presence is required, the business must be conveniently located, so employees and managers could be split into small groups to work in the business's geographically scattered branches. Under these circumstances workers might be unable to specialize to the extent that workers in a centrally located business might. Employees could be needed to perform several tasks, and branch managers could be expected to oversee operations, personnel, marketing and other functions.

The customer's presence also means that the business must pay attention to the aesthetic and functional aspects of the physical facility. The premises must not only be conducive to getting the work done, but they also must look inviting, attractive, professional, comfortable, clean and modern. The appearance and demeanor of other customers and employees are also of concern.

Customers' participation in providing the service means they must be able to perform their roles comfortably, willingly and accurately. The facilities should be laid out logically and sequentially so, for example, fast food customers will know where to enter the queue, place and pick up their order, pay, find condiments, sit and dispose of their trash. Signage to assist customers must be prominently displayed and understandable. Contingency plans need to be in place for customers who may have special needs or requests, be new to the service, resist playing their roles or make mistakes in doing so.

Customers' interaction with employees means that employees might be cast in several roles. Workers must be technically competent to do their jobs, but their interpersonal skills are highly relevant also, because these traits affect customers' willingness to cooperate, satisfaction, perceptions of quality and repeat patronage. Service businesses that work hard to develop the interpersonal skills of customer-contact employees might find that more employees could benefit from such training. For example, guests at Disney-World often ask park sweepers for information rather than employees in designated informational booths.

Customer-contact employees also may find themselves in marketing-relevant roles such as sales and marketing research. Employees should be knowledgeable of the company's services because customers can make requests that could lead to sales of additional services. Any worker should be able to make the sale or refer customers to the correct department. These customer needs, observations of customer behavior and customer inquiries and comments can be valuable forms of marketing research if systematically recorded and analyzed.

If employees' jobs are defined too narrowly, if their supervisor's scope of responsibility is confined to operations or if there's a separate marketing or sales department in the company, customer-contact employees are not likely to capitalize on the marketing potential of their customer encounters. They might decide that it's not their job—and if you haven't included customer service in your job description, they'd be right.

THE SERVICE SYSTEM

Every service business has a system in which equipment, materials, facilities, employees, customers, processes and structure all come together to create the service. The infinite number of ways in which these elements are arranged and sequenced can dramatically affect operational efficiency, service quality, customer perceptions and employee satisfaction.

Typically, small business owners do not formally and comprehensively design and plan the service system. Rather, the initial system is usually copied from other businesses or intuitively patched together. Over time, the entrepreneur or management team may fine-tune the service system as the business grows, as technology improves, as customers' tastes change and as additional experience with the system accumulates.

One helpful tool used to plan and diagnose the service system is the service blueprint. In much the same way as an architect might use blueprints to outline plans for a building, a service entrepreneur may develop blueprints to weigh service system options and to communicate the system to others.

Sample Blueprint for Auto Rental Agency

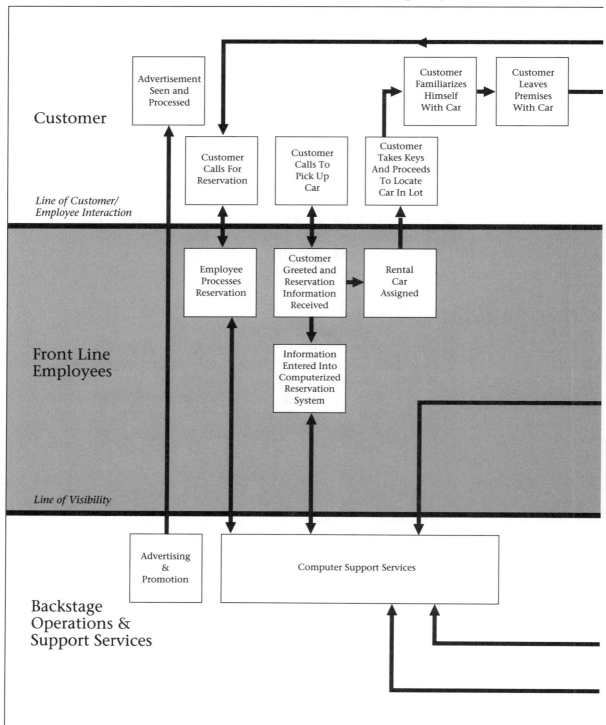

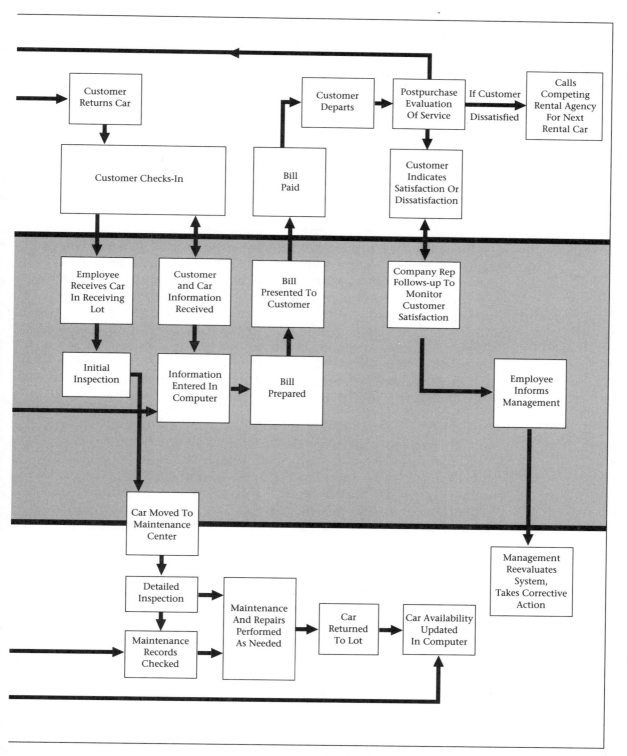

In its simplest form, a service blueprint resembles a flow-chart that illustrates the chronological processes, activities and people involved in the service system. The flowchart could be scanned from left to right so readers grasp the order of the steps. On the left side of the flowchart, the service customer begins the process by contacting the business to make a reservation after seeing the company's ad. Employees schedule the customer and prepare the car. The customer arrives and interacts with employees who, in turn, interact with other employees to provide the service. The flowchart could show a network of options to match the customer's requirements with service options. After the customer's departure, follow-up and reporting steps may be required.

More complex blueprints integrate the service process with the business structure, identifying, for example, times when employees interact with customers or other employees, which activities are performed in view of customers and which are performed backstage and how support and management functions contribute to the service process. A blueprint also might indicate where in the physical facilities each step takes place and the duration of each step. The blueprint on pages 76–77 illustrates the service system for an auto rental company.

New service businesses could develop several blueprints and evaluate each one. Existing businesses could benefit from blueprinting the system and then evaluating it for possible modifications to increase the system's capacity; identify training needs; and make the system more cost efficient, customer-friendly, flexible, faster, accurate and controllable. In communicating the service system to supervisors and workers, the blueprint can be helpful in showing how each job or department affects both the entire organization and its customers. The following questions might be raised in the process of diagnosing the service system blueprint.

▶ What are the skills and qualifications needed for each worker at each step? What sort of training is needed at each step? Which step might benefit most from the cross-training of employees?

► Which steps are most critical to customer satisfaction? How can satisfaction be enhanced at these points?

► At what points do customers interact with employees? What sort of impression do the interactions leave on customers? How can the quality of those interactions be improved?

► At what points are customers expected to participate in the creation of the service? Should the level of customer participation be altered? How effective are customers in their roles, and what might be done to enhance their effectiveness (improved signage, employee assistance, instructional manuals, etc.)?

► At what points do customer-contact employees interact with other employees? How can the quality of these interactions be improved?

► In what ways can the system best accommodate the introduction of a new service? Should the system be modified to accommodate the new service?

► How can the process be streamlined or simplified? Should some steps be eliminated or combined?

► Where can automation be introduced to speed service or reduce the likelihood of human error?

► How and where is service quality monitored? Should additional controls be introduced?

► What questions or comments are customers likely to raise during each step of the process? How should they be addressed?

► What decisions do employees have to make at each step in the process? What sort of training or information support systems might help employees with these decisions?

► How long must customers wait at each point in the process? If the waits are intolerable, what can be done to shorten them or alter customers' perceptions of their length (for example, entertain customers, give customers something to do)?

► What steps are most likely to result in deviations from established standards? Which steps create the most dissatisfied customers?

► What are the capacity constraints? Should resources be reallocated to alleviate bottlenecks?

► How quickly can employees contact a supervisor or manager at each point in the system?

► What are the chances and the consequences of service failures (for example, equipment malfunctions or employee absence)? How can such failures be avoided? Are adequate contingency plans in place to cope with these failures when they do occur?

Your Turn

Practice blueprinting by charting your experience the next time you dine out. The first step might be an encounter with a sign that instructs you in some way (Please wait to be seated). Interactions with employees should be noted as well as where the encounters took place, how much time elapsed during each encounter, whether you felt comfortable throughout the process, what tasks you performed and what tasks employees performed during each encounter. Developing and scrutinizing blueprints from the customer's point of view helps to reinforce the importance of designing the business around customers rather than forcing customers to accommodate the business.

DESIGN AND STRUCTURE

Organizational design and structure issues pertain to the business's division of labor, domains of responsibility and reporting relationships. There is no single type of organization that is best for all service businesses. The ideal organizational design and structure hinges on the nature and number of the services provided, the desired degree of customization or standardization, the amount of customer-contact required, the skills and experience of managers and employees, the expectations of customers and the size of the business. Because all of these factors may change over time, the appropriateness of any particular organizational structure is also subject to change.

However, given the challenges faced by service businesses, one general guideline can be offered: "Flatter" organizations with few layers of management are usually preferable to taller pyramid-type ones. Communication tends to flow more smoothly in flatter organizations. Management is more likely to understand and support employees and know what transpires on the front line between employees and customers, and front-line employees are more likely to know what is expected of them. Because decision-making authority is closer to the front lines, flatter structures enable service employees to be more responsive to customers, and response time can be shortened. This flexibility and timeliness is critical in serving today's service consumers.

Line Organizations

In a very small service business, the line organization may work well. The owner tops the chart and all employees report directly to him or her. As the business grows, employees may report to one or a few supervisors or managers, at least in the owner's absence. As the business continues to grow, a line organization becomes increasingly cumbersome. Other types of organizations emerge.

Example of a Line Organizational Chart

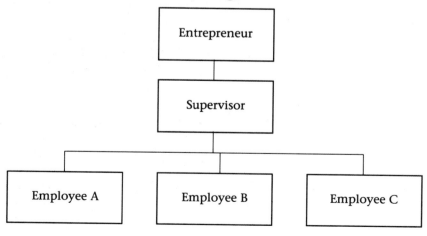

Functional Organizations

Many companies organize along functional lines with re-sponsibilities assigned to departments such as operations, accounting and finance, marketing, human resources (per-sonnel), purchasing and others. Managers and employees may push for such an organization because their educa-tional training and work experience may be concentrated in one functional specialty and they may have little interest in any other area.

Example of a Functional Organizational Chart

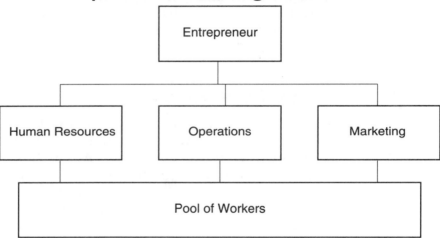

Although a functional organization is commonly and effec-tively used in manufacturing businesses, it may not work well at the branch level of service businesses because functional tasks are tightly interwoven and require the coordination and integration that separate managers or departments may be unable to provide. Personnel, operations, customer service and marketing decisions affect one another so closely that formalized efforts to separate and control the four functional areas may not be practical. For example, the marketing department might make advertising claims that the opera-tions staff cannot honor because human resources cannot recruit and train qualified workers. Moreover, employees might need to perform more than one functional role simultaneously, but workers' job effectiveness and morale are jeopardized if they report to separate managers. At the opposite extreme, employees could neglect roles outside of the domain of their immediate supervisors.

Decentralization

What is typically needed at the individual location level is a highly qualified, experienced unit manager responsible for multiple functions—someone who will not lose sight of the big picture, who will orchestrate necessary tasks and who will communicate priorities and objectives to front-line supervisors and workers.

If the business is large enough to have several locations, it might be useful to provide staff support services such as packaged advertising, promotional tools, signage, training manuals, marketing research, computer software, supplies or payroll services from headquarters. Ideally, unit managers should retain some latitude in using these services. Otherwise, managers may not enthusiastically embrace corporate mandates.

Example of a Multisite Decentralized Organization

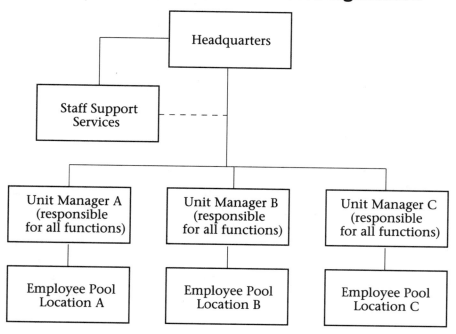

Specialization

In many consumer service operations, entry-level employees perform highly specialized and somewhat routine tasks. In effect they become partitioned by functional boundaries. A bank teller may process deposits and withdrawals. Bank customers who want an auto loan, credit card, IRA or other service may be referred to other employees, each of whom specializes in a limited range of the bank's services. The advantages of this sort of specialization are increased efficiencies: Employees' productivity increases as they learn to perform their job tasks quickly, accurately and with little training. If the service is highly standardized, well understood by customers, in sufficient and consistent demand and performed out of customers' view, a high degree of specialization may be appropriate.

Example of Functional Specialization at Lower Levels in the Organization

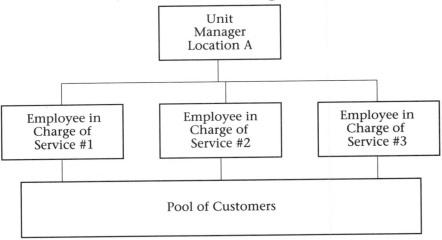

However efficient for the business, too much specialization may prevent the business from customizing service to suit consumers' individual preferences. Neither the system nor employees may be able to fulfill nonroutine service requests. In addition, too much specialization may interfere with building relationships with customers. Overly specialized employees may focus more on their specific job tasks than on customers. If each of several specialists encounters one customer briefly, none of them might learn and use the customer's name, establish rapport or understand his needs.

When employees fail to connect with customers, sales opportunities are missed and sales leads dropped. The bank employee who specializes in auto loans could process a customer's loan application without realizing that the customer also might be interested in a checking account or credit card. The loan officer may not think to ask if the applicant needs other bank services, the customers may not feel comfortable asking, or the customer may perceive the required contact with another employee as too much of an inconvenience.

Relationship Building

Cross-training employees serves multiple customers needs and avoids passing the customer from one employee to the next. For example, a bank employee might be trained to provide several services for a specific list of customers. The banking relationship is nurtured as customers develop trust and confidence in their personal bankers and look to them as expert sources of banking services.

Example of a Relationship-Building Organization

```
                        ┌──────────────────┐
                        │   Unit Manager   │
                        └──────────────────┘
                                 │
         ┌───────────────────────┼───────────────────────┐
┌──────────────────┐   ┌──────────────────┐   ┌──────────────────┐
│  Case Worker A   │   │  Case Worker B   │   │  Case Worker C   │
│  (responsible    │   │  (responsible    │   │  (responsible    │
│  for all services)│  │  for all services)│  │  for all services)│
└──────────────────┘   └──────────────────┘   └──────────────────┘
         │                       │                       │
┌──────────────────┐   ┌──────────────────┐   ┌──────────────────┐
│    Customers     │   │    Customers     │   │    Customers     │
│   1 thru 100     │   │  101 thru 200    │   │  201 thru 300    │
└──────────────────┘   └──────────────────┘   └──────────────────┘
```

Designated Customer-Contact Employees

If the services are too numerous or too technical for one employee to represent all of them to the customer, a specific employee still could be designated to interact with the customer. That employee then works with other employees or departments to coordinate the service and manage customer communications.

This sort of organization helps customers to feel comfortable, increases the likelihood of cross-selling additional services, minimizes the likelihood of customers receiving conflicting information from different employees, shields customers from employees with inadequate interpersonal skills and puts a specific employee in charge of monitoring and building relationships with a specific set of customers. In organizations without such designated employees, unhappy customers may come and go without any company representative ever learning of their dissatisfaction or being held accountable for customers' continued patronage.

Example of an Organization with Designated Customer-Contact Employees

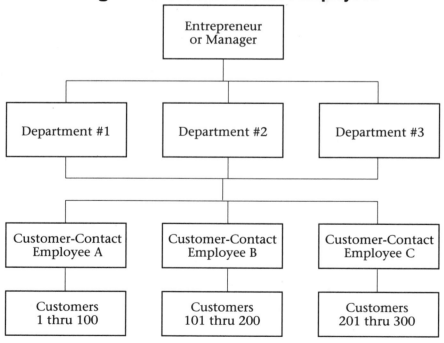

Team Approaches

Still another organizational twist in service businesses is that of employee work teams. Such teams may be essential to providing highly technical services (such as surgery) that require many skills. In addition, the collective wisdom of teams of employees with different viewpoints and experiences is often effective in identifying concepts for new services, improving the service system and overhauling company policies.

Organization by teams also makes sense for many routine tasks or services provided on a minute-to-minute basis. Teams provide a support system for less experienced employees and a form of peer pressure to elevate the performance of more experienced workers. Teams provide a social network that reduces stress and introduces teammates to a broader range of tasks that stimulate employee development and prevent burnout. Teams give employees a psychological boost by fostering a sense of belonging and teamwork even could translate into improved service quality. One study asked employees if their organizational unit was meeting service standards. Those who admitted their units were not performing up to par also tended to disagree with statements such as these.

► I feel that I am part of a team in my unit

► Everyone in my unit contributes to a team effort in serving customers

► I feel a sense of responsibility to help my fellow employees do their jobs well

► My fellow employees and I cooperate more than we compete

► I feel that I am an important member of this company*

---

*Berry, Leonard L., Valarie A. Zeithaml, and A. Parasuraman (1990), Five Imperatives for Improving Service Quality, *Sloan Management Review*, 29(Summer), pp. 29–38.

Example of a Team Approach to Organization

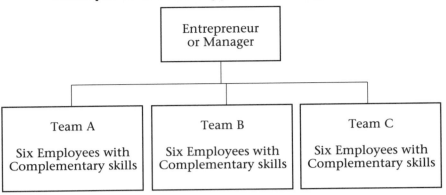

Teamwork can be fostered in several ways. One approach is to cross-train employees so they can gain a broader perspective of the entire business operation, develop a specific appreciation for coworkers and help one another during rush periods.

Evaluating and rewarding teams of employees, rather than individuals, is another way to encourage employees to work together. Instead of recognizing the Employee of the Month, honor the Team of the Month, or let employees select a Team Player of the Month to recognize coworkers who are most cooperative and supportive of their teammates. Other ways to promote teamwork include:

▶ Designate team performance goals

▶ Hold group meetings and training sessions in which employees work together to address challenging issues

▶ Encourage social outings or recreational activities away from the job (for example, form a bowling team or league)

▶ Hold receptions to welcome new employees

▶ Celebrate employee birthdays and

▶ Provide lounges or other areas where employees can congregate during breaks.

Your Turn *Find a copy of the organizational chart for a service company you know. As practice, redesign it to improve the efficiency and effectiveness of the operation. Consider how interactions between front-line employees and customers or between employees or departments may differ. How might the reorganization affect customer satisfaction, employee morale, productivity and teamwork?*

SUMMARY

Decisions regarding organizational issues can have a dramatic impact on how the service is delivered, how productive employees are and how workers interact with one another and with customers. In most service businesses, these decisions should reflect customers' presence, their interaction with service workers and, in many cases, their self-service role in providing all or part of the service themselves.

Service blueprinting is a particularly useful diagnostic tool to portray the processes and structure of the service system. Service blueprints show the sequence of the steps involved in delivering the service and the points of contact between employees and customers. Scrutiny of the blueprint can lead to modifications that streamline the number of steps, reduce customer waiting time, improve the quality of interactions between employees and customers or identify training needs.

Organizational charts show how the business designates responsibility and to whom employees, managers and staff are accountable. The organizational structure for very small service firms may be informal and flexible. Although the structure may vary from business to business, keeping the structure flexible as the business grows is a worthwhile objective because the marketplace changes constantly and the functional areas such as marketing, operations and human resources are interdependent.

ASK YOURSELF

▶ The service system can usually be designed in several ways. Before adopting one for your service business, design several and compare them. Could the best parts of each option be combined to offset their weaknesses?

▶ Share copies of your service blueprint with employees. Ask them how the service process might be improved.

▶ After you launch your service business, periodically review the need for reorganization. Has the business outgrown the usefulness of the existing organizational design and structure?

CHAPTER
NINE

UNDERSTANDING
SERVICE
QUALITY

QUALITY DOESN'T COST— IT PAYS

Improving quality is a concept that has begun to transform corporate America. Large and small companies alike are formalizing quality programs. Slogans have become more than advertising hype: They have found their way into corporate mission statements and planning documents. In many cases they have become part of corporate philosophies and cultures. Even companies that have not formally adopted quality development programs have come to understand the vital role that quality plays in successful, competitive businesses.

The rise of the corporate quality movement partially stems from increased competition in the marketplace. For most businesses, efforts to raise quality standards promise greater cost efficiencies, improved employee morale, more satisfied and loyal customers and ultimately greater profitability. As competition intensifies in both manufacturing and service industries, companies with only mediocre quality will find it difficult to thrive, or even to survive. Marginal quality simply is not acceptable in today's competitive marketplace.

Service Quality Commitments

Quality is still our recipe.
   —Wendy's

Service that can't be duplicated.
   —Pitney Bowes Copier Systems

When you preach quality, you'd better practice it.
   —Florida Power & Light

Quality in everything we do.
   —Ernst & Young Accountants

Expect more from us.
   —Chemical Mortgage Company

On time, every time.
   —Contel Communication Systems

America's most satisfied customers.
    —Wheaton Van Lines

Good enough isn't good enough.
    —Metropolitan Life

You don't just rent a car. You rent a company.
    —Hertz

Studies have shown that quality pays off. One study contrasted the performance of firms whose service quality was rated among the top third in their respective industries to that of firms whose service quality was rated in the bottom third.* The findings were dramatic. High-quality firms achieved an average sales growth of 17% compared to 8% for lower-quality firms. Return on sales was higher for the high-quality firms (12% versus 1%), as were prices relative to competitors (7% versus –2%) and changes in market share (6% versus –2%).

THE SERVICE QUALITY CHALLENGE

While all businesses should be concerned about quality, the quality issues facing service businesses are different from those faced by manufacturers. Most significantly, human behavior plays a much more central role in service quality than in manufacturing quality. The differences are evident from the perspective of service customers, employees and managers.

For customers, verbal and nonverbal behaviors of front-line service workers are noticeable, and those behaviors affect customer satisfaction. In contrast, customers may never know anything about the workers who assemble their household possessions.

---

*Thompson, Phillip, Glenn Desoursa, and Bradley T. Gale (1985), The Strategic Management of Service and Quality, *Quality Progress,* (June), p. 24.

Service workers are challenged by the infinite number of customers they serve. Different customers can expect different levels of service, and the differences are not always apparent. A waiter in a restaurant may serve two parties with equal promptness, but one group may feel rushed while the other feels ignored.

It is difficult for managers to measure the quality of an intangible, and often it is unrealistic to supervise every employee-customer encounter. As a result, defective services can be delivered to unsuspecting customers. To some extent, assembly-line service operations reduce the number of technical errors in the service, but the human interaction that many customers value may be sacrificed. Rigid step-by-step procedures for employees to follow may help to standardize the service, but this approach may leave employees powerless to satisfy customers with varying tastes who don't want such cookie-cutter service.

Managing human behavior is an inescapable ingredient in service quality programs. Service quality is likely to vary from employee to employee and may vary from minute to minute for the same employee, but it is not easy to standardize behavior when every employee brings different baggage to the job. Some workers have more or different skills than others. Some are more easily trained and motivated; others resist supervision and are easily frustrated. Some tire more quickly than others or are easily shaken by irate customers. Some service workers have their own ideas about what constitutes good service, and some are wrong.

WHAT IS SERVICE QUALITY?

Service quality refers to the evaluation of the overall excellence of a service. As applied by individual businesses, however, it is apparent that service quality means different things to different people. To some businesses, service quality has a technical, objective meaning, such as consistently adhering to performance specifications. Some business leaders prefer a more subjective, customer-driven definition, such as putting customers' interests first; others think in terms of their business's performance compared to the competition's.

All three of these perspectives are legitimate and not at all contradictory. Adherance to standards or specifications implies that some thought has been given to what the requirements should be and how they should be measured. If quality—like anything else—isn't measured, businesses will never know if they have achieved it. Putting customers' interests first is admirable because it suggests that customer input helps shape service standards or specifications, as it should. Finally, service practices and norms established by competitors are relevant as well, because these benchmarks help to shape customers' expectations and perceptions of quality.

Ten Components of Service Quality

In the mid-1980s, researchers at Texas A&M University launched an ambitious series of studies to investigate service quality.* Their research has involved a wide variety of service consumers and service managers from several service businesses.

The initial phase of the research revealed 10 key components (or "determinants") of service quality to help businesses refine their commitment to improving service. These components include:

1. *Reliability.* Being dependable and performing consistently, getting the job done right the first time and keeping promises; not surprising the customer with service mishaps or excuses.

2. *Responsiveness.* Providing the service in a timely manner and willingly assisting customers.

3. *Competence.* Having the skills and knowledge necessary to perform the service.

---

*Zeithaml, Valarie, A., A. Parasuraman, and Leonard L. Berry (1990), *Delivering Quality Service.* New York: The Free Press.

4. *Access.* Being approachable and convenient. Examples: Staying open during customer-convenient times, answering the telephone or promptly returning calls.

5. *Courtesy.* Ensuring that customer-contact staff is friendly, polite and respectful.

6. *Communication.* Keeping customers informed, listening to customers. Examples: Letting customers know in advance that prices or operating procedures will change; explaining service without using unnecessary technical jargon.

7. *Credibility.* Keeping the customer's best interests in mind; being trustworthy, believable and honest.

8. *Security.* Ensuring customers are free from risk, doubt or physical danger. Examples: Keeping account information confidential, providing well-lighted parking lots.

9. *Understanding the customer.* Learning the customer's needs and preferences. Examples: Salesperson asking about customer's interest in the service and reasons for buying before pitching a specific service.

10. *Tangibles.* Managing the appearance of the service facility and of customer-contact employees. Examples: Cleaning premises, upgrading the decor, establishing dress code for employees.

 *Your Turn*

Identify at least three possible service standards in your business for each of the 10 components of service quality. For example, one standard for the access component might be to answer the telephone within three rings. A possible standard for tangibles might be to sweep and mop the floor daily. Before formally adopting these standards, ensure that they are consistent with what customers say is important.

The Technical and Personal Dimensions of Service Quality

Some of the 10 components of service quality are central to a technical or procedural side of service (for example, the *what* dimension, shown on page 99). These include reliability, responsiveness, credibility, security and especially competence. Other components are more closely related to *how* employees interact with customers. Personnel represent the personal side or the how dimension (access, courtesy and communication). The remaining components (understanding the customer and tangibles) relate to both dimensions.

The goal is to excel on both the procedural and the personal dimensions, but some service businesses perform poorly on one or the other. Unfortunately, some excel at neither, but often it is the personal side that's neglected or left to employees' common sense. To illustrate, a 1987 article in *The Wall Street Journal* reported that American corporations typically invest only $2.58 per employee to improve their dealings with the public (March 17, p. 1). A recent study shows one of the devastating consequences of ignoring the personal dimension of service quality:

> Only 10% of all referrals were found to be cases where technical considerations or results were given as the reason for the referral. Fully 90% of all the reasons given for referrals were related to the [personal dimension]. (Source: *Managing the Professional Service Firm*, New York: The Free Press, 1993, p. 81)

Also recognizing the importance of both dimensions of service quality, another expert has characterized types of service businesses according to their combination of quality on both dimensions.

Dual Dimensions of Service Quality

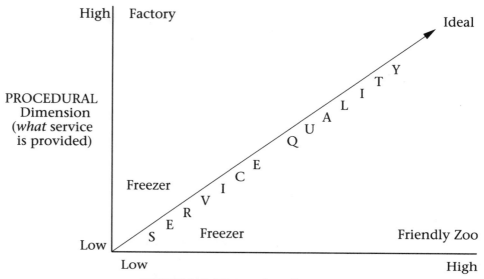

- ▶ *Freezers.* These service firms rate low on both dimensions, in effect signaling to customers: We don't care.

- ▶ *Factories.* These may rate high on the procedural dimension but low on the personal side. They tell customers: You are a number. We are here to process you.

- ▶ *Friendly Zoos.* These rate high on the personal dimension, but low on the procedural one. The message they convey: We are trying hard, but we don't really know what we're doing.

- ▶ *Ideals.* These rate high on both dimensions. Their message: We care, and we deliver.

Source: *Quality Service: The Restaurant Manager's Bible,* William B. Martin, Ithaca, NY: Cornell University, 1986, Chapter 7.

SUMMARY

Businesses that deliver superior quality service tend to be more profitable and grow at a faster rate than businesses with mediocre or poor quality. In recent years, more service organizations have recognized this quality-success relationship.

The term service quality means different things to different people: meeting specifications, beating the competition or consistently high performance. Ultimately it is the customer who defines what service quality is, and it is the customer who notices when it is absent. Quality service consistently meets customers' expectations.

Research suggests at least 10 components of service quality that are highly relevant to customers: reliability, responsiveness, competence, access, courtesy, communication, credibility, security, understanding the customer and tangibles. These components can be categorized into two dimensions of quality—technical or procedural, and personal. These two dimensions highlight the notion that service quality is a function both of what service is delivered (the technical dimension), but also how the service is delivered (the personal dimension).

ASK YOURSELF

▶ How important is service quality to you as a customer? As an entrepreneur?

▶ How do your customers define service quality in your type of business? Specifically what aspects of quality are most important to them? Have you asked them?

▶ If you are already operating a service business, ask your employees what they think service quality is. Are their perceptions consistent with your own and with those of your customers?

▶ How does the service your business provides compare to that of your chief competitors? Would your customers agree with your assessment?

CHAPTER
TEN

MANAGING
SERVICE
QUALITY

MEASUR-ING AND MONITOR-ING SERVICE QUALITY

Firms that deliver quality service are those that consistently meet or exceed customers' expectations. Some service businesses that fall short of meeting their customers' expectations are not fully aware of what those expectations are. Others have difficulty interpreting data from customer surveys and formulating a service action plan.

The first step to improving service quality is knowing how service quality rates. It is not enough to know that the business is profitable or that revenues are on the rise. By improving service quality, the business could become even more profitable. Further, customer retention is not always an indicator of service quality. Customers may continue to patronize the business even when quality is marginal, if they feel they have no other choice. Such marginal quality and lack of customer choice are ripe conditions for competitors to enter the marketplace.

Customers should play a central role in evaluating service quality, but that doesn't necessarily mean they should specify the standards, per se—especially if the processes used to develop the service are highly technical and not well understood by customers. However, customers can specify the results they would like to see, and they know how they would like to be treated. This input may be used to redesign the service system and establish specifications to meet those customer preferences. For example, customers may not care how many telephone operators are on duty, how much training those employees have or what type of information support system is used, but they may be able to specify the promptness with which the phone should be answered when they call and how quickly their inquiries should be answered.

Keeping tabs on competitors' service quality is a good idea. Their quality levels may be on the rise so that an ambitious service quality program may be needed to compete. Entrepreneurs preparing to start service businesses are advised to measure competitors' level of service quality to know what levels of service customers have come to expect.

Service quality can be evaluated in several ways. Some are more formal or scientific than others, and some are more expensive than others. Most of them evaluate service quality through customers' eyes. Each method has its advantages and weaknesses, so it is better to use a combination of methods. Let's examine a few of the most common measurement approaches.

SERVQUAL

SERVQUAL—short for SERVice QUALity—is a fairly sophisticated and scientific scale for measuring customers' expectations of quality and their perceptions of the business's quality performance. The SERVQUAL scale measures overall service quality, which can be very helpful in seeing how much service levels progress by month or year. However, the scale is not very useful for identifying specific service glitches or isolated mishaps that managers may need to know about right away.

For a copy of the scale and a detailed explanation of its development and use, call or write the Marketing Science Institute (1000 Massachusetts Ave., Cambridge, MA 02138, telephone: 617-491-2060). Ask for report number 86-108, "SERVQUAL: A Multiple-Item Scale for Measuring Customer Perceptions of Service Quality."

Focus Groups

Focus groups are a useful way to get in-depth customer comments about service quality. Small groups of customers (usually six to 10) meet with a manager (or ideally an unbiased, independent moderator) to have a focused discussion of the business's service quality. Focus groups can tap both customer expectations of what the level of service quality should be as well as customer perceptions of what the service quality is.

Focus groups can be held with part-time or new employees whose perspectives may be fresh and more like those of customers than those of long-time employees or managers.

Such focus groups help to identify quality problems, and employees often suggest solutions and recommend ways that management can support their efforts. Involving employees in focus groups boosts morale by helping them to feel more professional and a valuable part of the service team.

Although focus group data is not easily quantifiable, it is often rich with detail. The issues identified in focus groups may be framed as specific questions and placed on formal surveys to generate more quantifiable data that is easier to track.

Follow-up and Debriefing Sessions

Customers sometimes are hesitant to speak up on their own, but many will offer feedback if specifically asked. So, make it a point to ask. For routine, low-cost services, a follow-up phone call may be sufficient. For more involved services, a face-to-face debriefing session may be in order. Begin with general questions, such as: Were you happy with our service? What suggestions might you have to help us improve our service? If the customer seems hesitant or vague, be more specific: Did the employee handling your account explain the service that was performed and the accompanying charges? Was the work completed promptly? Were we easy to do business with? Additional quantified feedback may be obtained by leaving a survey or evaluation form and asking the customer to complete it and mail it back to the company.

Customer Comment Cards

Customer comment cards are typically about 4" × 6" cards made available to customers at the service facility. The cards ask a few questions regarding customer satisfaction and quality perceptions. An example of a question might be:

How happy are you with today's _____
(cleanliness of facilities, courtesy of personnel, promptness
of service, etc.)?

- ❏ Very pleased

- ❏ Somewhat pleased

- ❏ Somewhat displeased

- ❏ Very displeased

Focus groups or some other form of research should be used first to identify the most relevant service characteristics to be included on the cards. A few blank lines may be included to capture additional comments that don't fit the predetermined categories. Sometimes a few other questions are asked to help classify the answers, pinpoint the causes of problems, hold employees and supervisors accountable and follow up. Examples: location of the business (for chain operators); date and time of visit; service purchased; name of service provider; customer's frequency of patronage, age, gender, name and address (usually optional).

Comment cards can identify specific mishaps or instances of outstanding service, but because only a few customers bother to fill them out (typically fewer than 5%), they may not accurately measure the quality of the service normally provided. That's why it's a good idea to offer an incentive to encourage a wide range of customers to fill them out.

Consumer Hotlines

Toll-free consumer hotlines can be more customer-convenient than comment cards, and they offer an alternative for customers who may not be able to express themselves clearly in writing. On surveys and comment cards, for example, irate customers simply may remark: The service is lousy. Vague comments like this one provide little direction for the business. One of the advantages of hotlines is that they enable call-handlers the opportunity to probe for additional, specific information. Well-trained call-handlers can give customers immediate feedback—such as an apology or promise of a refund—that may soothe customers' frustration.

Some customers may prefer to offer comments anonymously and therefore avoid using the hotlines. Like comment card systems, comments voiced on the hotline may not be representative of most customers. In addition, the expense of staffing a hotline with trained employees may be significant. Trying to minimize these expenses may result in mishandled calls or comments missed altogether when calls are not answered.

Mystery Service Audits

Monitoring employees when they interact with customers is difficult. Even if the technical or procedural level of quality can be assessed, the personal dimension may go unsupervised. Mystery service auditors address this problem by posing as customers. They may check to ensure that transactions are handled properly, that questions are answered correctly and that employees act courteously.

The findings of mystery service audits may be used to reward outstanding employees, to identify employee training needs and to uncover snags in the service system that may be beyond the control of service workers. The findings may be surprising and revealing. For example, audits of bowling centers across the country indicate these discouraging employee tendencies.*

▶ Before visiting the bowling centers for the first time, auditors called the centers to inquire about location, prices and operating hours. Only 25% of the employees handling these calls thanked the mystery bowlers for calling.

---

*Martin, Charles L. (1990), The Employee/Customer Interface: An Empirical Investigation of Employee Behaviors and Customer Perceptions, *Journal of Sport Management*, 4(January), pp. 1–20.

- Only 45% of service desk employees expressed a welcoming greeting when mystery bowlers arrived at the bowling centers.

- When mystery bowlers approached the snack bar, employees in 42% of the audits were preoccupied with noncustomer tasks that delayed service. After serving the auditors, only 54% of the employees thanked the bowlers.

- When auditors reported minor problems (e.g., empty paper towel dispenser) to service personnel, only 14% of the employees thanked the auditors for reporting the problem and only 35% apologized for any inconvenience it may have created.

- During the 90-minute visits to the bowling centers, only 10% of the auditors were asked to join a bowling league, bowl in a tournament or bowl in specific events.

- After auditors paid for three lines of bowling, 64% of the service workers in these encounters thanked the auditors, and only 21% asked or encouraged the bowlers to visit the business again.

Unconditional Service Guarantees

As many as 96% of dissatisfied customers never voice their complaints to the business. Of complaints that are voiced, many are stifled by employees who never relay the complaints to supervisors. When managers don't hear very many complaints, they conclude that service quality must be okay and that customers are satisfied. But dissatisfied customers may not step forward because they fear entering into an unwanted confrontation or because they believe that complaining won't change anything or that the time and effort required to voice complaints isn't worth it.

Unconditional service guarantees help to address this problem by offering customers an incentive to speak up when they are dissatisfied and by calming customers' fears of confrontations with defensive or unempathetic employees. If the guarantees are in the form of certificates or other sort of paper trail, management can track the number of times the guarantee is invoked without having to rely on voluntary reports from employees.

Employee Surveys

Customers might define service quality, but employees control it and know what they need to deliver it. Their experience serving customers makes them a valuable source of information. Moreover, employees' enthusiasm for service quality generally has a lot to do with the way they feel about their jobs. Service quality will suffer when employee morale suffers.

American Airlines is one service firm that routinely surveys employees. It probes nine factors: company image, job satisfaction, supervision, operating effectiveness, fairness, feedback, participation, advancement opportunity and communication.

Day-to-Day Contact

You can do all these things to monitor service quality, but there is no substitute for day-to-day involvement in the business. This means spending time in the service facility performing routine tasks, serving and listening to customers, making employees feel comfortable in your presence and chatting with suppliers about your quality goals and how they might be able to help. These experiences are valuable sources of feedback and insight, so resist the temptation to hide behind a desk. Instead, routinely schedule time on the front-line—where the action is—and insist that the entire management team does the same.

PROBLEM DIAGNOSIS: USING THE DATA

It may flatter customers and employees to have their feedback solicited, but the greatest value of service quality evaluations is realized when the data is analyzed and used to improve service. At the very least, discussions should be held with employees and supervisors to share the data and explore possibilities for action. Several tools and techniques can help plan and conduct these meetings, including gap analyses, service blueprinting, frequency distributions and data stratification, and causal chains and fishbone analyses.

Gap Analysis

This approach has gained popularity among service organizations although there's nothing new about the basic concept. Gap analysis examines differences or gaps between measurements that should be aligned. The type of gap and its magnitude provide some direction for action.

The most critical gap is the one between customers' expectations and their perceptions of service. When expectations exceed perceptions, there's a dissatisfaction gap. Closing the gap involves lowering customer expectations, raising customer perceptions or some combination. Keeping score on this fundamental gap can give employees and supervisors some sense of progress.

Another useful gap to examine is that between customers' expectations of service and management's (or employees') estimates of customer expectations. Movie theater patrons may report that the most important service features of the theater are quiet audiences, safely lit aisles and comfortable seats, but if management wrongly assumes that pastel toilet paper in the restrooms, movie previews and chocolate-flavored popcorn are the most important features, initiatives to provide quality service may be misdirected.

Service Blueprinting

Blueprinting the production and delivery of the service facilitates a critical analysis of how the system might be simplified, automated, speeded up, made less confusing or more personable to customers, or otherwise improved. Which steps in the process are the most error prone? What steps might be added to improve service quality? At what points in the process are employees most likely to interact with customers, and how can those interactions be enhanced? At what points are supervisors most needed? Blueprints also help to show employees how their jobs fit into the big picture and how their work quality affects that of other employees or customer satisfaction.

Frequency Distributions and Data Stratification

These tools help to identify hidden problems that otherwise may be averaged away. For example, a bank's customers may report waiting in line for an average of two minutes, and they may find two-minute waits to be acceptable. However, if the data were collected for hundreds of customers, several may report intolerable waits of 10 minutes or longer. Looking only at the average (two minutes) conceals the dissatisfaction experienced by some customers.

A frequency distribution would show the number of customers reporting waits of varying lengths of time (for example, 18 customers waited five seconds or less, 26 customers waited six to 15 seconds, 31 waited 16–25 seconds). Data stratification breaks out the data by branch location, day of the week, time of the day or other factors in an effort to identify when, where and why the longest waits occur.

Causal Chains and Fishbone Analyses

Sometimes customers will identify what they view as problems, but it may not be possible to address the reported problems directly. The customers' concerns may be symptomatic of other problems that can be solved. A football fan's observation that the home team would win more games if it scored more points than its opponents might be accurate, but not directly actionable. What has caused the team to score fewer points? Airline passengers may complain that flight departures are delayed too often, but that problem requires further analysis to be actionable. Causal chains and fishbone analyses can help.

Using the simpler causal chain technique, one would ask: What causes flights to be delayed? If late-connecting flights are the primary reason, one might then probe to learn that mechanical failures cause connecting flights to be late, which in turn are caused by improper maintenance procedures. At that link in the causal chain—improper maintenance procedures—the root of the problem can best be addressed.

A fishbone analysis is similar to the causal chain except that multiple causes are considered. The symptomatic problem (such as delayed flight departures) is diagrammed as a fish spine, from which extend a network of bones related to possible causes (such as procedures, personnel, equipment, materials or other reasons).

FINALIZING THE SERVICE QUALITY ACTION PLAN

Scrutiny of the service quality data in conjunction with analysis tools should point to areas of improvement. The next step is to assemble and implement an action plan. Like any business improvement plan, let workers know you are serious about service quality by formulating quantifiable goals and setting deadlines for reaching them, by assigning responsibility for achieving results and by introducing an incentive and reward system to get employees excited about the plan. Here are some suggestions from the Texas A&M researchers.

► *Manage customer expectations.* Never overpromise. It is better to exceed realistic promises than to fall short of unrealistic ones.

► *Manage the evidence.* Attend to the details of the appearance.

► *Educate customers about the service.* More informed consumers interact better with employees, they know how to access the service and they usually make better decisions. Thus, they are more likely to be satisfied with the service.

▶ *Develop a quality culture.* Every employee must buy into the quality concept, and they must be able to perform. This means selective hiring, continuous training and monitoring/motivation of employee performance.

▶ *Leverage the freedom factor.* Empower employees with enough flexibility to address unique service circumstances when they occur.

▶ *Automate quality.* Where possible, replace error-prone human employees with technology.

▶ *Follow-up the service.* Make sure the service was performed satisfactorily. Make it convenient for customers to contact the business when it is not.

▶ *Be great at problem resolution.* When an inevitable mishap occurs, address it promptly and to the customer's satisfaction.

Another set of complementary principles and recommendations for improving quality has been suggested by the National Institute of Standards and Technology (of the U.S. Department of Commerce) as part of its guidelines for the annual Malcolm Baldrige National Quality Award.

▶ Quality is defined by the customer

▶ Senior leadership must create clear quality values and build the values into the way the company operates

▶ Quality excellence derives from well-designed and well-executed systems and processes

▶ Continuous improvement must be part of the management of all systems and processes

▶ Companies need to develop goals and strategic and operational plans to achieve quality leadership

▶ Shortening the response time of all company operations and processes needs to be part of the quality improvement effort

▶ Company operations and decisions need to be based on facts and data

▶ All employees must be suitably trained and involved in quality activities

▶ Design quality and defect and error prevention should be major elements of the quality system

▶ Companies must communicate quality requirements to suppliers and work to elevate supplier quality performance

More information on the Baldrige awards and these quality-related concepts may be obtained from the N.I.S.T. at Route 270 and Quince Orchard Rd., Administration Building, Room A537, Gaithersburg, MD 20899 (Telephone: 301-975-2036).

ASK YOURSELF

► How many customers or prospective customers have you talked to today? What did you learn about service quality from those discussions?

► How do your views of service quality differ from those of customers and employees?

► Of the eight approaches that may be used to measure or monitor service quality, which would be the most appropriate in your business? Consider: Which are the most quantitative? Which involve employees? Which are the most (and least) expensive to implement? Which are the most (and least) time consuming?

► Interpret the following statement: Service businesses should seek to increase the number of customer complaints it receives.

► Have you included service quality as an integral part of your business planning process? What should be the major components of your service business's quality improvement action plan?

CHAPTER
ELEVEN

PERSONNEL
POWER

THE SERVICE PERSON- NEL CHAL- LENGE

Most service businesses are fundamentally people businesses. The interaction between customers and employees lies at the heart of service transactions and relationships. What front-line employees say and do is vitally important to customer satisfaction, service quality and ultimately the success of the service business.

All employees are vital to the success of any business, but the role played by front-line service workers is magnified. As far as customers are concerned, service employees not only provide the service on behalf of the business, they *are* the service and they *are* the business.

Service businesses cannot afford to staff customer-contact positions with inexperienced, inadequately trained employees, but all too often, that's exactly what they do. And when they do, the businesses and their customers suffer.

The most successful service organizations work diligently to find top talent. They invest in training and employee development. They support employees with the equipment, processes and information needed to perform their jobs. To a degree, they design jobs to fit employees, rather than demanding that employees fit the requirements of the jobs. They solicit input from employees as aggressively as they solicit information from customers. They listen, and they trust workers by letting them make decisions. Let's examine some of these human resource issues more closely.

RECRUITING THE BEST

Recruiting employees is like recruiting customers. In fact, jobs are among the most important products people buy. While most service entrepreneurs recognize that attracting new customers involves more marketing savvy than posting Customers Wanted signs or placing classified ads in the newspapers, many entrepreneurs will settle for such passive efforts to attract job applicants. Such lackluster efforts may have been appropriate years ago when service jobs required fewer skills and the number of qualified applicants exceeded the number of job vacancies, but competition for today's talent pool is much more intense.

Because the ideal job candidate is more likely to be found in a pool of 30 or 40 applicants than in a pool of two or three, employers need an aggressive, systematic approach to attract a sufficient number of qualified applicants. That means creating jobs that prospective employees will want and communicating their availability.

Desirable Jobs

The best candidates view the most desirable jobs as interesting and challenging with opportunities for personal and professional growth. One study conducted by the Roper Center for Public Opinion found that 62% of surveyed workers rated job security as essential to job satisfaction.* The same study found career advancement opportunities to be essential to 56% of the respondents, so attracting and retaining employees creates pressure for the business to grow to create these opportunities for workers.

The Roper study also found that half of the surveyed workers deemed it essential to use their initiative on the job. This concern for creativity and flexibility was especially important to newer workers. In response, service businesses are working to streamline the rulebooks and empower their employees to use personal judgment when faced with unusual circumstances or customer requests. Empowered employees may be authorized to spend up to a certain amount of money to placate dissatisfied customers, knowing that resolving customer complaints on the spot is more likely to make customers and employees happy than prolonged bureaucratic procedures.

Accompanying the interest in job security, initiative and career opportunities is an increased interest in compensation, employee benefits and other job enhancements. A 1975 study conducted by the Institute for Social Research at the University of Michigan found that 48% of high school seniors rated "Having a job that provides you with a chance to earn a good deal of money" to be very

*Waldrop, Judith (1991), Meet the New Boss, *American Demographics,* 13(June), pp. 26–32.

important. Follow-up research conducted 13 years later posed the same question to the class of 1988 and found that even more seniors (62%) reported that high-paying jobs were very important.* Another study found companies using employee benefits and job enhancements to compete for top talent (employee benefits can drive labor costs up by 30%–40%). Here's a sampling of the percentage of firms offering specific inducements in 1990 compared to those that plan to offer them by the year 2000.

Job Benefits and Enhancements	Offered in 1990 (%)	Will offer by 2000 (%)
Subsidization of child-care expenses	12	52
Sick-child facility/home-based care	3	28
Subsidization of elder-care expenses	3	23
Long-term-care insurance	8	68
Mentor/career counseling	29	67
Part-time employment	80	94
Flextime	52	86
Job sharing	24	67
Telecommuting	15	52

Source: International Foundation of Employee Benefits Plans, Brookfield, Wisconsin

Spreading the Word

Equipped with attractive service jobs and profiles of ideal candidates, service entrepreneurs should use multiple recruiting methods to attract applicants. One need not rely on traditional Help Wanted signs or classified ads. Fast food restaurants use colorful table tents and placements to advertise. The on-site ads stress the fun, challenge and excitement of working in the food service industry. Managers believe that existing customers make good employees because they are already familiar with the business and enjoy the food.

---

*Russell, Cheryl (1993), The Master Trend, *American Demographics*, 15(October), pp. 28–37.

Other options abound. Offer incentives to employees for recruiting qualified applicants. Talk to guidance counselors and placement officers at local high schools and colleges. Ask them to steer qualified applicants your way, or advertise in the schools' newspapers—promising part-time positions, flexible working hours and tuition assistance benefits that students find appealing. Participate in a career fair at which candidates can gather information about the company and the available jobs without the pressure of the formal interview. Employment agencies are another alternative. Private agencies often charge a fee, but they often have a large pool of applicants from which to draw, and they provide helpful and time-saving services such as background checks and skill testing.

SCREENING THE APPLICANTS

Not every applicant will be equally qualified, so they will need to be screened and evaluated. The nature of the job has a lot to do with the screening process. Some applicants may be well suited for some positions, but not for others. Some may have the technical skills needed to perform well on behind-the-scenes jobs, while others have valuable human relations skills that would enable them to work well with customers. One study of large firms noted for their exemplary customer service identified universal competencies that outstanding customer-service professionals possess. These desirable characteristics include the ability to build customer loyalty and confidence; ability to empathize with customers; effective communication skills, including active listening; ability to handle stress and mental alertness. Personal motivation and a high energy level also were found to be desirable applicant traits.*

In some instances, a new job could be created, an existing job redesigned or existing workers redeployed to accommodate the aptitudes and skills of an outstanding applicant who otherwise might not represent a good fit with current

---

*Lessons From Top Service Providers, Stamford, CT: Learning International, 1991.

job vacancies. The alternative of not hiring such an individual may be unacceptable. That is, the applicant may prove to be a valuable employee for a competitor!

If workers' jobs are interrelated and complex, suggesting that teamwork is essential, workers and supervisors should be involved in sifting job applications. If the existing team can participate in the screening and evaluation process, they will be more committed to working with the new hires, making them feel welcome and helping to make them successful.

If the vacancies involve a lot of customer contact, past experience in working with the public usually is desirable, and, of course, interpersonal skills are a must. Interview questions concerning past job experiences may reveal whether candidates are articulate and can think on their feet, but they also may indicate if they are team players and customer-oriented ("My coworkers were the greatest. I really enjoyed working with them, but we had some annoying customers who would interrupt our work with silly questions.") If telephone skills are needed, stage a brief telephone interview by asking applicants to call the following day to reiterate their interest in the job.

Specific attitude scales and psychological tests may be administered to assess candidates' honesty, personality, racial prejudices, reactions to stress and other job-relevant traits. Some of these tests are publicly available in local libraries, and others are available through commercial testing centers.

One useful scale was published in the *Journal of Personality and Social Psychology* (Vol. 30, No. 4, pp. 526–537). It measures behavioral flexibility; that is, applicants' ability to adapt from one situation or customer to another. Here is a sampling of five of the scale's 25 true or false statements (responses indicating behavioral flexibility are included in parentheses).

1. I find it hard to imitate the behavior of other people. (False)

2. My behavior is usually an expression of my true inner feelings, attitudes and beliefs. (False)

3. At parties and social gatherings, I do not attempt to do or say things that others will like. (False)

4. I can make impromptu speeches even on topics about which I have almost no information. (True)

5. When I am uncertain how to act in a social situation, I look to the behavior of others for cues. (True)

ORIENTATION OF NEW HIRES

The first few days on a new job can be stressful for new service employees. Their stress may stifle their enthusiasm for the new job and cause service quality to deteriorate. The newcomers' relationships with customers, coworkers and supervisors may suffer. Their confidence may erode.

Orientation programs can greatly reduce new employees' stress level. The orientation is separate from job training and should be used to provide new hires with an overview of the operation and to show them how their jobs fit into the grand scheme of things and affect other departments, employees and customers. The company's philosophy of business should be described at this time, conveying a service vision. Specific job training will teach them what to do, but this part of their orientation will help to clarify why they do it, thereby elevating their commitment to superior performance.

Company benefits and personnel policies should be explained during orientation. Does the company have an insurance plan? Who should employees call when they are sick? When is payday? The detail may be overwhelming, however, so much of the information can be included in an employee handbook, including opportunities to ask questions. Be sure to include opportunities for new hires to ask questions.

If the business facility is large, a physical tour might be included as part of the orientation. Such tours not only help to orient employees, but they also enable employees to orient customers and visitors. The offices of other employees and departments should be included as part of the tour, especially those most closely connected with the new employee's job. The layout of the facility may not be obvious, so it should be clarified during the tour. For example, the sequence of offices down the hall might correspond to the flow of paperwork associated with the service. The location of restrooms, coffee lounges, telephones, water fountains, supply cabinets, time clock, employee parking and other features of personal interest also should be pointed out. Include safety features— entrances and exits, fire alarms and extinguishers, first aid kits, electrical circuit breakers, maintenance supplies (for example, mops to clean spills), burglar alarms, and so on.

In addition to acclimating new employees to the physical environment, new recruits also need to be acclimated to coworkers. Introductions to other employees, semi-formal receptions and pictures or notices posted on the company bulletin board or printed in the company newsletter help to welcome new employees, make them feel like valued members of the team and makes others in the organization seem more approachable.

TRAINING AND DEVELOPMENT

Every worker needs training to ensure that service standards are communicated, understood and followed. For customer-contact employees, training is doubly important because misspoken words or other mishaps can go undetected and may be irretrievable once they happen.

In addition to training's obvious benefit of developing employee competence, training also serves to instill employee confidence; a sense of professionalism; and commitment to the job, company and customers. Well-trained workers are more productive because they waste less time and materials in performing tasks accurately the first time. Coordination and teamwork increase as well, as trained employees see how their jobs fit into the big picture and as they learn new ways to help their coworkers. Scheduling flexibility is another benefit; cross-trained workers may be able to switch between several jobs as needed. Well-trained employees can identify new ways to make operations more efficient or more effective, and they are positioned to increase customer satisfaction; customers notice the differences trained employees make.

Despite the benefits of training, not all training programs are equally effective. Here are a few common training pitfalls.

▶ Putting new employees on the front line too quickly, leading some customers to wonder if it is their job to train employees.

▶ Training exclusively on either the technical or human relations dimensions of the job, but not both.

▶ Focusing on imparting knowledge, but not on developing skills. Suggestion: Give employees a chance to practice skills with role playing and hands-on exercises.

▶ Establishing training as an event, rather than as a continuous process. Suggestions: Continually challenge workers by exposing them to new training programs. Reward employees who respond to training opportunities. Reward supervisors and managers who are effective, teaching-oriented coaches.

▶ Instructing employees what to do and how to do it without explaining why to do it. Suggestion: Work toward empowering employees with a short list of specific job objectives rather than overwhelming them with long lists of job tasks.

▶ Relying solely on employee reactions to evaluate the effectiveness of training. Suggestions: Administer a quiz to measure learning. Observe employees to ensure that they are applying the training to their jobs. Check their work output to ensure that the desired results are achieved.

► Not supporting or reinforcing the training on the job. Suggestions: Make sure supervisors are familiar with the training program and that they take it seriously. Ensure that the work environment is supportive. Are the tools, equipment, supplies, time and information available to enable workers to perform their jobs as trained?

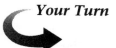

Your Turn   **To learn more about available commercial training materials, browse through training-related trade journals at your local public library. Contact the advertisers in these magazines for more information about the training tools they offer. Crisp Publications has a catalogue of books and videos used in training: 1-800-442-7477.**

EMPLOYEE COACHING AND SUPERVISION

Rather than abandoning new employees once the initial training program is complete, the most successful service organizations continue to work closely with inexperienced employees who may need to work near their supervisors or more experienced employees. Newer workers should be provided with immediate feedback to reinforce the training program and to fine-tune job skills. The first few weeks on the job are critical to establish good work habits.

As employees' experience grows, coaching and direct supervision may be supplemented with less obtrusive methods. Automation, reporting and other control mechanisms may be used to monitor employee performance and productivity; periodic feedback can be established to enhance both. For example, electronic cash registers might tally total sales for each employee, the number of customers sold, the size and composition of each order and the number of service guarantees honored. The phone system may be equipped to compute the number of calls handled and the duration of each call. Initialed paperwork provides a record of service activity that can be scrutinized after the service is performed or periodically spot-checked. Ensure that the adopted performance measures and standards are appropriate and consistent. For example, an operational standard of handling incoming telephone calls in 60 seconds or less may be incompatible with sales standards of booking reservations for at least 50% of all callers. Less formally, customer-contact employees may be tempted to neglect customers if their supervisors hand them long lists of chores unrelated to serving customers.

Since customers have more contact with employees than supervisors, customers can be involved in monitoring and motivating employees. Mystery customer auditors may be authorized to reward employees who demonstrate specific behaviors such as using the customer's name, thanking the customer or smiling. Periodic surveys and comment cards should ask customers to name outstanding servers or evaluate the demeanor or responsiveness of employees. Employee recognition contests may be staged in which loyal customers are mailed coded vouchers with instructions to present them to employees who provide exemplary service. Employees honored with the coupons then redeem them for cash awards and prizes. (Award levels should be adjusted to reflect that some jobs involve more customer contact others.)

EMPLOYEE MOTIVATION

Highly motivated employees are those who maintain an intense and persistent effort to perform well on the job. Motivated employees are conscientious. They are mentally alert, energetic, enthusiastic and continuously seek ways to improve their productivity and performance. They care. Needless to say, motivated employees are an asset to any service business.

What does it take to stimulate or encourage employees to be motivated? There are dozens of motivational tools and most successful service firms use several. Some techniques are more effective for some employees than for others, and most employees respond best to a combination. Don't rely too heavily on esoteric theories of motivation—simply ask employees what motivates them. They may not always know precisely what drives them, but their thoughts are often much more accurate than the guesswork of others.

Employee empowerment may be the best motivator of front-line personnel, because it demonstrates a high level of respect for employees. Moreover, giving employees the authority and latitude to use their own judgment often leads to improved decisions, more satisfied customers, greater cooperation between employees, and workers who are better prepared to assume additional responsibilities. Too many rigid rules and policies can discourage employees, leading them to feel like dispensable pawns in a game of business chess.

Respect for employees also may be demonstrated by supporting employees with the tools and information they need to excel; soliciting their input on matters that affect their jobs and the business; recognizing their outstanding accomplishments and consistently high levels of performance; bragging to customers and the media about their skill, professionalism and dedication; nurturing rapport between workers, supervisors, and managers; and providing long-term career opportunities.

The effects of compensation as a motivator are debatable. While an attractive salary may help to recruit the top talent and discourage them from leaving the company, pay is not necessarily a strong motivator on a daily basis. However, the potential of future earnings in the form of pay raises, bonuses, sales commissions and job promotions could be highly motivating—especially if employees clearly perceive a direct link between service standards, effort and compensation.

Heightened motivation on a daily basis often involves efforts to help employees combat fatigue, stress and boredom. Not only are employees likely to lose their motivation when these symptoms arise, but they are likely to make mistakes as well, which both the business and customers pay for. Consequently, don't let employees perform only one task for too long, face too many customers, work alone all day, feel rushed or perform too many physically demanding chores. Cross-training employees so they can periodically rotate out of these demotivating situations not only helps to refresh them, but it also facilitates scheduling flexibility and fosters teamwork.

SUMMARY

Because service businesses tend to be labor intensive, their success often hinges on the ability and enthusiasm of employees. The innovativeness of the service concept, the experience of the founder, the attractiveness of the physical facilities, and the catchiness of the promotions amount to very little if service personnel is incompetent. Interpersonal skills are especially important for workers whose interaction with customers often defines the quality of service.

Preparing employees for the service challenge begins with creative and diligent efforts to recruit highly qualified applicants to good jobs. The next step involves screening to ensure that applicants have the right balance of technical, interpersonal and critical thinking skills, along with a high level of motivation. Once hired, employees may greatly benefit from a formal orientation program to acclimate them to the organization, work environment and their coworkers. Employee training is essential as well, because customers perceive employees as both the service and the business and because it is not always possible for supervisors to monitor and correct employees' work performance. Training should take place before new hires are exposed to customers. Additional training and coaching should contribute to employee development. Many motivational tools can have a dramatic effect on employee morale and customer perceptions. Empowering employees to deviate from rigid rules may be the most powerful motivator of front-line personnel.

ASK YOURSELF

► What does the following statement mean to you: As far as customers are concerned, service employees not only provide the service on behalf of the business, they are the service and they are the business.

► Why would some service managers lament that it is difficult to find qualified and highly motivated employees these days?

► Before putting together your human resources plan, recall your experiences as an employee working for someone else. What could the business have done better to orient, train, motivate and support you?

WELCOME TO THE SERVICE SECTOR

THE SERVICE PRICING CHAL-LENGE

Despite the necessity to set prices, the process of doing so is difficult. The ideal price for services may fluctuate daily depending on the state of the economy, what markets are served and what competitors do. In addition, knowing what to charge for services is difficult for several other reasons. Costs are often indirect so it is not always clear what prices must be charged to cover costs. Competitors may charge a wide range of prices that may not cover their costs. Customers may resist high prices if they do not understand or value the service, or they may resist low prices if they equate low price with low quality. Charging the wrong price at the wrong time can contribute to excessive swings in demand, resulting in undesirable periods of wasted capacity or capacity insufficient to meet the demand.

Pricing decisions can be improved by considering eight sets of factors. (A ninth set of factors is government regulation. Because regulatory issues are so industry- and community-specific, they will not be discussed here. Contact regulatory agencies, trade associations and the local chamber of commerce for information about pricing regulations that may apply to your service business.)

- ► Costs
- ► Market demand
- ► Competition
- ► Objectives
- ► Systems prices
- ► Nonmonetary prices
- ► Customer beliefs and expectations
- ► Pricing communications

COSTS

Entrepreneurs don't need degrees in accounting to know that the business's costs must be covered to make a profit. Despite the popularity of cost-based approaches to setting prices, determining precisely what a unit of service costs can be a subjective decision. Take labor, for example. If the service is highly customized—such as many professional and repair services—the precise amount of labor needed to produce it may not be known with certainty. Taking the time to reduce the uncertainty by diagnosing the service needs before beginning the work may be an extremely time-consuming task in itself, so many service providers pass along the risk to customers by charging a flat hourly rate. Understandably, customers often dislike such pricing practices.

Another labor costing problem arises when employees perform duties that are not directly traceable to a specific order or unit of service. In a fast food restaurant, for example, employees may spend about the same amount of time each day cleaning the grill and sweeping the floor, whether 100 or 1,000 burgers are sold. Because employees must be paid for these necessary yet indirect activities, it is difficult to assess how many burgers should account for these expenses. The cost-per-burger calculation will be higher if based on 100 burgers rather than 1,000 burgers.

When most of a service business's costs are indirect and don't fluctuate proportionately with volume, the difference in the range of cost allocation possibilities can be substantial. In movie theater operations, if a theater served only one moviegoer per day, the costs per customer would be so staggering that the price charged would drive away the customer. On the other hand, if the theater proprietor views the costs of serving the first customer each day as fixed, then the remaining variable costs per customer may be only a few cents. In this latter case, the theater might decide to offer discounts to large groups during nonpeak showings, conceding that recouping variable costs and a portion of the fixed costs is preferable to empty seats that generate no revenue whatsoever and cover no costs at all. This cost phenomenon can lead to a wide range of prices and intense competition among service businesses.

In the long term, of course, both fixed and variable costs must be covered. Otherwise the company will have insufficient funds to grow, modernize the physical facilities or otherwise invest in the business's future. Clearly, continuously operating on a short-term basis can have devastating results.

EXAMPLE

Suppose your service business's variable costs are 30 cents per unit and your normal price per unit is $2.50. Let's say that customers ordinarily purchase only one unit of service per day. Suppose some prospective customers are willing to commit to two units of service each on a specific day that's normally a low volume day—if you are willing to lower your price to $1.35 per unit on that day. If you refuse to grant their request for a price reduction, they will probably commit to only one unit of service each at the regular price. Should you accept their reservation and grant the price discount?

Answer: Economically, the options are similar, but keeping the higher price would be slightly more profitable. At the normal price of $2.50, the revenue contribution to fixed costs and profitability is $2.20 ($2.50 – .30). At the reduced price, the contribution per unit is lower, only $1.05 per unit ($1.35 – .30), but because each customer's volume promises to be double the ordinary volume, the contribution per customer also would be doubled to $2.10. Other considerations may come into play as well, making the decision less clear. For example, if you refuse to grant the discount, could all of the group's business be lost to the competition? If the discount is granted, might full-paying customers be turned away, or will other customers learn of the discount and demand a similar deal?

MARKET DEMAND

Another key pricing consideration is market demand. How much will customers pay for the service? Customers usually don't know and don't care what it costs the business to perform the service, so regardless of costs, service businesses must deliver value to customers if they are to survive. It makes more sense to determine how much customers would pay for a service and then design the service to keep costs in line, rather than determining costs first and then figuring out how to convince customers to pay enough to cover the business's costs.

Examining the customers' consequences of not purchasing the service is often a useful approach for estimating the upper limits of what customers might pay. For example, a creative entrepreneur in New York represents his clients in traffic court to argue for reduced fines. With a few exceptions, the fees must be less than the amount of money saved by the reduced ticket. Otherwise traffic offenders might as well go ahead and pay the full amount of the traffic fines. Likewise, a customer of an appliance repair shop probably would not pay more than the price of a new toaster to have an old toaster repaired.

Test markets are tools that manufacturers routinely use to help gauge market demand and refine pricing decisions. Different prices of a grocery store item, for example, might be tried in a few selected cities before the product is rolled out nationally. Differences in sales volume attributed to differences in price enable manufacturers to pinpoint the most profitable price. Traditional test markets may not be feasible for many services, especially when competitors are poised to steal the service concept and beat the original developer to the market. However, focus groups, surveys and tightly controlled laboratory test markets may be used to solicit customers' reactions to different price levels. One statistical tool, called conjoint analysis, could be used to weigh possible trade-offs between combinations of higher prices and extra features.

COMPETITION

Competitors typically mediate the gap between the lowest possible prices charged (based on costs) and the maximum possible prices (based on market demand), so it's worthwhile to check competitors' prices and evaluate their services continuously. In doing so, you can search for ways to add value to your own service or otherwise distinguish your business so that customers will not perceive any of your competitors as substitutes. Since competitors are probably trying to distinguish themselves as well, the reality is that customers may perceive a broad range of competitive choices. For example, to varying degrees amusement parks compete against dozens of other leisuretime and entertainment industries ranging from golf courses and arcades to home video rental stores. Customers are themselves competitors if they have the skill, equipment, time and inclination to provide the service themselves.

The need to reevaluate your prices continuously against those of your competitors is partially offset by the intangible nature of services and the fact that competitors are often geographically dispersed. Prospective customers may find it difficult and inconvenient to weigh prices and value across different service providers. They may compare only a few options, or if they have established a strong relationship with a particular service provider, they may not bother to compare prices at all.

OBJECTIVES

Every service business is different and every management team has a different vision for the future. Not surprisingly then, pricing decisions should reinforce the broader strategic, operating, marketing, financial and other objectives of the business. Pricing decisions should not be made in a vacuum.

Prices may be set to help the business accelerate cash flow (for example, pay promptly for a 2% discount) or generate additional revenue (Call our toll 1-900 number for technical support). Low prices may be used to drive away competitors or to minimize the likelihood of their entering the market. Discount prices may be used to attract new customers, such as when cable TV operators waive their normal installation fee. Prices may be used to shift demand from one period to another, such as when telephone companies vary their long distance rates throughout the day. Higher prices may be used to suggest a higher level of service quality or to cultivate a clientele that is not overly price sensitive. Continuity or frequency pricing may be used to reward loyalty (buy 11 and the 12th one is free). Price bundling may encourage larger volume purchases (Burger, fries and a medium drink for only $1.99). Price couponing may enable the business to appeal to price-sensitive customers without sacrificing full price customers.

SYSTEMS PRICES

The systems price is the total price the customer pays to acquire and use the service. It may be greater than the price received by the service business. A patient's trip to the physician may entail an office charge of $50, but the systems price also might include drugs the doctor prescribes, lost wages or babysitting expenses for the patient's children, parking and transportation. Students are keenly aware that the systems price of attending college extends far beyond the tuition and fees paid at the beginning of each school year. Room and board, books and supplies, photocopying and other clerical expenses, transportation, sporting and social events and other expenses drive up the systems price.

In some instances the systems price may be high enough that customers are relatively insensitive to price increases. For example, ticket prices at DisneyWorld have increased dramatically since the early 1980s, but Disney still attracts thousands of guests for whom ticket prices represent only a small fraction of the total cost of their Florida vacation.

For less discretionary services, businesses sensitive to their customers' systems price plight might be able to command a premium price for their services if they can offset other parts of the systems price. For example, it may be practical to extend the business's operating hours or speed up service so customers won't be forced to lose time on their jobs to acquire the service. A few other examples might include babysitting services, parking, delivery or transportation and food service.

NONMONETARY PRICES

Augmenting the systems prices are nonmonetary prices; that is, prices other than money that customers pay. These include lifestyle prices (membership in a health club may require a commitment to exercise), sensory prices (discomfort caused by dirty, unsanitary restrooms) and place price (inconvenient location). Two of the most significant nonmonetary prices to examine more closely are time and psychic prices.

Time Price

Time is as much a currency for many customers as dollars, and time-hungry customers may eagerly exchange dollars for time. Customers may not perceive much of a bargain if the monetary price is low but the time spent waiting for service is high. The best bargain may be the service that frees customers' time for other purposes. Such time-saving benefits are the primary purchase motives for many consumers purchasing services such as maintenance services, Fax services, overnight package delivery services, fast food and one-hour photo development.

Psychic Prices

Psychic prices are the psychological feelings of anxiety, stress or discomfort associated with the service. In the early days of automatic teller machines, the banking community learned that many bank customers avoided ATMs because of high psychic prices. Some customers felt uneasy with the technology and were concerned that they might make errors that would wipe out their account balances. Other customers feared that ATMs might grant unauthorized access to their accounts, while others were concerned about potential robberies at the machine locations.

A physician's patients may fear the embarassment of disrobing or the pain of being stuck with a needle. They may worry about catching a worse illness from other sick patients, hearing bad news about their condition from the physician and, of course, the anticipated bill may arouse some anxiety. Customers of repair services may worry that the broken item won't be fixed correctly. The stay of hotel guests may turn sour if they experience a rude or otherwise unprofessional desk clerk. Lunch customers at a fast-food restaurant may worry that other customers may break in line or light cigarettes in a nonsmoking section. A woman may be concerned that her mother-in-law won't approve of her decision to place her newborn in day care. An attorney's clients may feel intimidated by incomprehensible legal jargon.

Recognizing that psychic prices can adversely affect customers, minimize the psychic prices they pay by making them feel as comfortable as possible. Unconditional service guarantees may reduce much of the anxiety. Friendly and courteous personnel also are helpful in this regard. Creating a relaxing atmosphere with pastel colors, soft music, coffee and donuts, magazines or other reading materials and ample space is a good approach. Establishing rapport with customers helps to alleviate some of the interpersonal anxieties, while keeping customers informed and being accessible helps to reduce the stress and anxiety associated with the unknown. Finally, consistent, fair and simple operating policies help to reduce psychic prices by eliminating anxiety-producing surprises and possibly giving customers a sense of control.

CUSTOMER BELIEFS AND EXPECTATIONS

Pricing decisions that clash with customers' beliefs and expectations could meet with resistance or unanticipated reactions in the marketplace. Tradition, past purchases and competitors' pricing practices shape these price perceptions. Purchasers of consumer durable goods, for example, may expect free delivery and installation services.

In the mid-1970s gasoline stations in many parts of the United States began pricing gasoline by the liter. Many consumers who were accustomed to paying by the gallon resisted liter pricing because they found it confusing to compare prices. For example, is $.31 per liter at one station a lower price than $1.22 per gallon at the station across the street? Eventually the liter stations reverted to pricing by the gallon.

Perhaps the most widely reported service belief or expectation is the perceived relationship between prices and quality. In the absence of nonprice information about the service, price often serves as an indicator of quality—the higher the price, the higher the quality.

Imagine this: an advertisement that claims: Complete upper and lower dentures for $250. I know nothing about that dental center except for the ads, so their dentures may be the best in the world as far as I know objectively. But whenever I see the ads, images of a seventeen-year old dental technician flash through my mind. He wears a blood-stained smock and approaches patients with a standard 12-inch ruler to take their dental measurements. "Looks like you'll need a medium sir," he says as he reaches into a large corrugated box (labeled M) and pulls out a pair. In my vision, he sometimes knocks the dust off the dentures by wiping them on his smock, but sometimes he just raises the dentures to his mouth and blows the dust off before handing them to dazed patients. Of course, if the patient's mouth is between sizes, the technician reaches for a nearby shoehorn. While there may be a very receptive market for such inexpensive dentures, I suspect I'll call a different dental center if I ever need to wear them.

In some instances, price-quality perceptions mean that customers may be fairly insensitive to price. Operators of a municipal swimming pool found that they attracted more swimmers on weekends when they raised admission prices substantially. Patrons believed that the higher prices somehow meant improved service in the form of more lifeguards, cleaner facilities or some other benefits.

Another consumer expectation is that prices will not be substantially higher the next time the service is purchased than it was the last time. Prior purchases serve as reference points to help consumers estimate what fair and reasonable prices are. Customers may experience sticker shock if they purchase the service infrequently, so communicate price information between purchases. Historical pricing might make it difficult to recover from deeply discounted prices. During the recession of the early 1990s, for example, several fast-food chains lowered prices on some menu items by as much as 30%. When the recession ended, customers did not accept restored, higher prices, so some of the discounts remain intact today.

This doesn't mean that discounting should be avoided, but it does mean that pricing reference points should be preserved so customers will remember what the normal price is. Rather than slashing prices by 50%, offer a two-for-one special instead. For a $20 service, the net discounted price is the same, $10, but two-for-one buyers are more likely to accept that the price will be $20 after the discount promotion ends.

PRICING COMMUNICATIONS

A comprehensive pricing plan should include some consideration of pricing communications to help manage customers' perceptions of price. Relevant questions include: What information will be communicated to customers about price? How will it be communicated? To what extent will price be emphasized as a competitive weapon? How will customer resistance to prices be handled?

First, accept the reality that there's almost always at least one competitor who can match or beat any price, so promoting the business solely on the basis of price is usually a mistake. Instead of talking too much about low prices, stress the service's added benefits, exclusive features, high quality and superb value. Mention the business's fine reputation, guarantees and experienced workers, but avoid pricing battles with competitors. To avoid competing solely on the basis of price is a good strategy in any industry, but it is especially so in service industries where costs are largely fixed and the intangibility factor makes it difficult for customers to evaluate and understand what they are getting for their money.

Another pricing reality for most service businesses is that no matter what price is charged, some customers will believe it's too high. Customers may find it difficult to evaluate intangible services, and they may not understand what services were provided when invoices are not explained and itemized.

Staff can present prices in a more favorable light by stressing the service's benefits, exclusive or hidden features and overall value, but they might not be trained well enough to respond to pricing complaints: Training service staff to break down the price into smaller increments often makes the price more palatable. ("$350 may seem like a lot of money to renew the insurance policy for another year, but it's really costing you less than $1 per day.") If inflation is the culprit, "the increase will enable us to continue to provide the top-flight service you deserve."

SUMMARY

Determining what prices to charge for services can be challenging. Relevant pricing considerations may be grouped into eight categories that serve as a checklist for establishing, reviewing and modifying prices. These pricing considerations include:

► *Costs.* What are the total costs involved in producing and delivering each unit of service? Which costs are fixed and which are variable?

► *Market demand.* What is the maximum amount customers would pay?

► *Competition.* How much do competitors charge for similar services or for suitable substitutes?

► *Objectives.* What are the business's primary objectives, and how can prices help to satisfy them?

► *Systems price.* What is the customer's total cost for purchasing and using the service? Could a portion be eliminated or offset?

► *Nonmonetary prices.* What do customers pay in terms of time and mental anxiety? Could some of these prices be alleviated to enhance customers' perceptions of value?

► *Customer beliefs and expectations.* How might customers' perceptions affect their reaction to pricing decisions?

► *Pricing communications.* How is price communicated to customers? Have employees been trained to handle complaints about prices?

ASK YOURSELF

▶ To establish initial reference points for pricing decisions, ask yourself three questions.

- What is the lowest possible price I can charge and still cover my costs?

- What is the most I can expect my customers to pay? The answer may vary for each group of customers served.

- What prices do my competitors charge?

▶ Have you considered each of the eight categories of considerations that may be used to determine price? In your business, which pricing considerations are most likely to change from month to month?

▶ As a consumer, think of a service business that offers high value at a reasonable price. How can it keep prices so competitive? Which pricing considerations seem to be most relevant to that business?

CHAPTER THIRTEEN

GROWING
THE
SERVICE
BUSINESS

THE SERVICE GROWTH CHAL- LENGE

One of the most exciting, challenging and rewarding aspects of owning and operating a business is watching it grow. Indeed, the dream of building a business empire is appealing to many entrepreneurs and is fueled by the successful growth stories of service firms like McDonald's, Wendy's, Federal Express, Marriott and Southwest Airlines, to name a few.

Watching the business grow, however, doesn't mean watching from the sidelines. A few entrepreneurial ventures may be lucky enough to experience short-term growth by hitting on the right concept in the right market at the right time, but long-term growth is no accident, and it certainly is not guaranteed. Growth takes foresight, planning and the willingness to make choices and accept the risks that accompany those choices. Growing the business is both a choice and a controllable set of options.

For service entrepreneurs, the growth challenge is magnified by two of the characteristics of services discussed throughout this book—intangibility and simultaneous production and consumption. Because services are intangible, they can't be shipped, so distribution options are severely limited. Rarely can service businesses rely on an established network of wholesalers, distributors and retailers to facilitate growth. For the most part, service businesses must distribute their services themselves or create a distribution system where none existed previously.

The intangibility factor also may impede growth in that entrepreneurs find it difficult to secure the capital they need to fund growth, especially the early stages of growth. Potential lenders and investors might get excited about a manufacturing venture after seeing a prototype, but they find it difficult to evaluate a service concept that may be little more than an idea—let alone forecast its sales and expected cash flow.

Simultaneous production and consumption usually means that the customer's presence is required, so most service businesses have to locate where the customers are. Growth may mean establishing numerous small neighborhood outlets rather than operating from one large, central location. Often the geographic dispersion contributes to control problems and may reduce the potential for operational economies of scale.

A manufacturer's customers may never see the plant or any employees, but a service business's plant and employees may be quite visible, and the impressions they make can be critical. High visibility can constrain growth opportunities for service firms if entrepreneurs cannot justify the diversion of management attention and other resources from existing operations to pursue growth.

BENEFITS AND RISKS OF GROWTH

The rewards of growing a service business can be tremendous, but there are risks, too. Personal and staff morale, marketplace leadership and the promise of enhanced profitability may be appealing, but personal preferences and limitations, the risk of neglecting existing operations, unstable new markets and the financial risk should be considered.

Morale

Growing a business to gain financial independence, fill a niche in the marketplace, create jobs in the community, or simply to build something from the ground up can be personally satisfying—a morale booster and motivator. Employee and management morale tends to be high in growing businesses as well, because growth creates advancement opportunities. Growing companies can attract, develop and retain quality workers, which provides a competitive advantage and builds a solid foundation for further growth.

Sometimes growth opportunities may be viewed as obstacles, inconveniences or threats. Some employees and managers are effective when the business is small, but they do not have the abilities to take the company to the next level of growth. Others may prefer the comfort of a routine, familiar job. Consequently, expect some workers to resist efforts to grow the business.

Marketplace Leadership

Growth positions the company as a leader or as an up-and-comer, creating favorable impressions in the minds of customers, suppliers, financial backers and future owners. As the business becomes well-known, customers may assume that quality is high. Suppliers may grant favorable treatment, not wanting to lose an account with such great potential. Bankers may offer to lend money after recognizing the business's great track record. When it is time to sell the business, prospective buyers will be more likely to pay top dollar if the business is still growing.

Personal Preferences and Limitations

The personal preferences and abilities of the entrepreneur may not mesh well with the characteristics of a growing business. Many small business owners prefer to keep their businesses small to maintain close relationships with customers and employees or to avoid financial risk, relocation, excessive travel, distasteful bureaucracies or other big-business trappings. Some simply prefer more free time and they recognize that growing the business can be time consuming.

Thinly Spread Resources

Growth may spread resources too thin, especially if it is too rapid or not well planned. For example, operations may suffer if owners and managers become too preoccupied with growth to attend to the day-to-day details of the existing business. Money that might otherwise be used to upgrade existing facilities may be diverted to fuel new opportunities. The quality of service may suffer as well, if personnel is not developed rapidly enough to staff the new operations. When resources are spread too thinly, the entire business may lose its credibility.

Greener Pastures

The pastures may not be greener on the growth side when it comes to new customers. Attracting and opening accounts for new customers can be more expensive than originally envisioned, and new customers may be too price-sensitive to be profitable. Serving newer customers often requires more time, but their purchase volumes generally are lower than those of existing customers. If new customers are drawn from new market segments and they share the same facilities with existing customers, problems of customer incompatibility could arise. For example, long-standing adult customers may resent a new Teen Night promotion.

Generally new customers are necessary for business growth, but the appeal of growing the business by attracting new customers (especially new customers in the same market area) should be balanced against the reality that it may take some time and money to convert them into loyal regulars.

Potential Profitability

The most apparent reason for pursuing growth is the promise of greater profits, but increased profits are not guaranteed by this route. Profits may increase from several sources including increased revenues, cost savings, time leverage and erosion of competition.

Revenues. Higher revenues usually mean higher profitability, although the rate of increase may not be proportionate. For example, a 10% increase in revenues may result in profits greater than, less than, or equal to 10%. Losses are also a possibility. The additional investment in facilities, personnel, equipment and marketing required to expand operations may elevate costs so much that a very significant increase in revenues is needed to realize any added profits. Moreover, revenue gains usually lag behind costs, so often businesses that grow too much too rapidly experience a serious cash flow problem. However, if variable costs per unit are low and most costs are fixed and barely fluctuate with changes in volume (such as costs for a hotel or movie theater), a slight increase in revenues can have a dramatic and positive impact on profitability.

Cost Savings. The initial cost structure for the business may be quite small. Many entrepreneurs originally operate the business from their homes and perform all of the work themselves so overhead expenses are low and payroll expenses nonexistent.

As the business grows, however, additional expenses and investments are piled onto the cost structure. Added facilities, personnel, equipment, financing and maintenance drive costs sharply upward when home-based businesses leave home and acquire new quarters. These costs, plus the costs of additional management, are added each time the business opens a new branch. Research and development costs may soar each time a new service is evaluated and added to the line. The intent of all these growth maneuvers is to capitalize on untapped demand, but growth costs become losses if demand fails to materialize.

Some cost savings may accompany the growth, although the savings typically are less in the service sector than they would be for comparable expense categories in the manufacturing sector. For example, prices for supplies and equipment may drop as purchasing clout increases. Promotion and advertising economies of scale may develop when the business expands in the same media market. Economies of scope may arise if the new service can use preexisting slack in the organization. For example, a savings and loan starting to offer car loans could use the same equipment, people, paperwork and financial analysis used in assessing the credit worthiness of home loan applicants.

Leveraged Time. In labor-intensive service businesses, growth usually facilitates the leveraging of profits by leveraging resources—in particular, the owner's or manager's time. Easy tasks requiring little skill may be delegated to low-paid and inexperienced workers; more difficult duties are earmarked for more skilled, more expensive workers. The challenge and risk lies in knowing which employees can handle which tasks. As the business grows, the founder might be able to increase profits by overseeing several branch managers using the same amount of time required to operate a single unit.

Although entrepreneurs often find it difficult to delegate duties as the business grows, efficiently matching each task's demands with the most appropriate workers keeps payroll costs in line, thereby boosting profits. Proper delegation also helps to develop personnel for future growth, and it frees the entrepreneur's time to pursue that growth.

Erosion of Competition. Competition is a fact of life for most service businesses, but it is rarely static. New competitors enter the marketplace and existing ones may pursue growth plans of their own. The decision not to grow often leads to a drop in market share, which eventually leads to an erosion of profitability or return on assets. This is especially true when demand is growing and the industry is expanding, but it also tends to hold true even if the size of the industry remains relatively constant.

Avoiding the negative consequences of nongrowth practically necessitates the pursuit of growth to some degree. Through growth, the business can discourage some potential competitors from entering the market and slow the growth of existing competitors. This increases the business's share of market demand, potential profits and future industry growth. A superior business concept may eliminate some competitors and the outright purchase of competitors certainly will.

GROWTH ALTERNATIVES

Once or if the growth decision is made, one or several interrelated growth options can be pursued. The risks and rewards associated with each alternative vary depending on the business, industry, marketplace and the ambitiousness with which the options are pursued, so it is impossible to say which growth option should be pursued first. However, the less risky options are found toward the top of the list.

- ▶ Financial management

- ▶ Increased purchase volume and frequency among existing customers

- ▶ Promotion to attract new customers

- ▶ Expanded or increased use of existing facilities

- ▶ Development or modification of service delivery systems

- ▶ Development of new services

- ▶ Addition of new locations

- ▶ Integration

Financial Management

Business growth usually means bigger operations, but profits also can be grown by managing the business's existing financial affairs. Moreover, getting the financial statements in shape helps to poise the business to capitalize on other growth opportunities and seek financing when needed. Expanded facilities or increases in sales growth, for example, are accompanied by a need for funds to finance the growth—funds that must be anticipated and made available when needed.

Start by comparing the business's financial performance with that of other businesses in the same industry. Knowing how the firm's sales, profits, assets, working capital and liquidity compare to competitors can be helpful in determining whether some financial adjustments should be made and whether competitors might be better positioned for growth. Trade associations can be useful sources of industry data.

Other sources to find this sort of information include *Annual Statement Studies,* published by Robert Morris Associates, and *Industry Norms and Key Business Ratios,* published by Dun & Bradstreet. Public libraries routinely carry these reference books. Before applying for a business loan, it may be a good idea to refer to these two sources. Lenders often consult these reference books. When they do, they may ask why your business is out of line with the rest of the industry.

A somewhat sophisticated use of service industry performance data has been developed by researchers at Western Michigan and Central Florida Universities.* They investigated financial management growth potential in the service sector and found that the typical service firm could financially sustain an annual sales growth rate of about 28%, in contrast to only 5% for manufacturers. Generally, labor-intensive service businesses were found to have higher sustainable growth rates than equipment-based service businesses.

A service business may use the estimated growth rate to gauge how rapidly the business should plan to expand sales, whether the rate of growth should be slowed or whether steps should be taken to improve the growth rate to accommodate growth plans. For example, the actions in the following list might be taken to increase the sustainable sales growth rate. Some of the actions involve cuts—tactics that may seem counterintuitive to growth, but that may be necessary to enable the business to take advantage of more profitable opportunities elsewhere.

- ► Increase prices to improve profit margins.

- ► Increase promotional efforts for the most profitable services in the line.

- ► Reduce expenses by cutting hours of operation.

- ► Tighten credit practices to minimize losses from bad debts.

- ► Eliminate less productive employees.

---

*Mayo, Edward J., and Lance P. Jarvis (1992), Excessive Growth in the Service Firm: A Strategic Marketing Planning Challenge, *Journal of Services Marketing,* 6(Spring), pp. 5–14.

- ► Reduce marketing efforts directed toward marginally profitable customer segments, unless they show strong potential for future profitability.

- ► Offer new services that yield economies of scope (that is, new services that can use existing assets and personnel).

- ► Prune the mix of services offered. Get rid of those that tie up assets and are only marginally profitable.

- ► Reduce the number of locations to free assets. Sell those that are not performing. Consider converting some to franchise operations.

- ► Engage in leasing. Sale and leaseback arrangements free up capital for growth.

- ► Eliminate duplicated and unproductive assets. Does each location or employee need the same range of equipment? Is some equipment rarely used? Can multiple locations share some of the same assets?

- ► Reduce inventories of supplies and maintenance items. For example, is a two-week buffer inventory really needed when suppliers ship within a few days?

- ► Reduce or eliminate dividends to free up funds for growth.

- ► Use standby lines of credit.

- ► Increase the debt-to-equity ratio by borrowing funds to fuel growth.

Increased Purchase Volume and Frequency Among Customers

Relationship marketing describes business efforts to strengthen ties with customers. The focus is on retaining and developing existing customers and stems from the realization that it is only marginally profitable, at best, to attract new customers if they can not be retained. The philosophy is analogous to filling a bucket with water (new customers) only to have the water leak through holes in the bucket. Rather than feverishly working to refill the bucket, businesses find it more profitable to plug the holes instead. Such an approach is particularly appropriate in mature or highly competitive service industries in which the pool of new customers is a shallow one.

Happily retained customers tend to be more profitable because they purchase more, are less concerned about price, are often easier to serve and they help to market the business by telling their friends and coworkers about how well they are treated.

Promotion to Attract New Customers

Although established customers tend to be more profitable than new customers, all customers were once new and some customers will be lost regardless of the business's efforts to keep them. Therefore, efforts to retain existing customers must be balanced against efforts to attract new ones. The objective should be to attract new customers that have a good chance of being profitably retained.

Start with prospective new customers that are most similar to existing, satisfied customers. Similar customers are more likely to be satisfied by the same service mix than dissimilar prospects would be, and they are more likely to get along with existing customers. The similarities may be based on demographics such as age, income, education, gender, or based upon customers' needs and expectations. Hotels, for example, have found that both demographics and expectations differ for business travelers and vacationers, so they avoid trying to appeal to both groups simultaneously.

Some situations would justify appealing to dissimilar market segments. One is when the pool of prospective new customers that is similar to existing ones is too shallow to satisfy the business's growth objectives. Sometimes the competition for customers similar to existing ones is too intense to be profitable. Third, the service system might be unable to accommodate more of the same type of customer if usage patterns also are the same. For example, a hotel operating near capacity during the week by catering primarily to business guests might promote getaway packages to attract tourists on the weekends.

Once you have decided which groups of new customers to attract, advertising and other promotional efforts may be used to steer the prospects toward purchase. Before you engage in an expensive advertising campaign, however, clarify your objectives.

Possible Objectives for Advertising of Services

► Create awareness of the business and the service by advertising key benefits or themes on a regular basis and by using the company name and the name of the service regularly

► Clarify the location of the business or where the service may be obtained

► Tell prospective customers who to contact for additional information

► Visualize the service by showing the equipment, building, or people used to produce it; displaying the company logo; using symbols to illustrate the service's benefits (AllState's good hands) or showing the outcome of the service (satisfied customers)

► Demonstrate the service or use before-after pictures or descriptions

► Strengthen customer relationships with emotional appeals, by emphasizing benefits of being a long-term customer, or by personalizing the message

► Promote quality by stressing the expertise of the service providers or other benefits of the service that may not be obvious, using testimonials of satisfied customers and offering unconditional service guarantees

- ▶ Leverage word-of-mouth communications by targeting gregarious opinion leaders; showing ad scenes with happy customers talking about the service; using humor, jingles or tongue-twisters and encouraging customers to contact the company (by promoting toll-free phone number)

- ▶ Manage customer expectations by explaining the service and promising only what is possible

- ▶ Enhance perceptions of value by explaining what the customer receives for the charge and the consequences of not using the service, breaking the price into smaller increments or conducting a value analysis

- ▶ Tell who the service is for to attract customers the business can serve effectively and increase the odds that customers will be compatible with one another

- ▶ Educate prospective customers about their role in the service process (a hospital might give patients a list of what to bring to the hospital)

- ▶ Reinforce employees' roles and responsibilities by bragging about their skills, commitment and professionalism

- ▶ Ask for the sale

Expanded Use of Existing Facilities

Sometimes a business can be grown by expanding capacity during peak times. This strategy can mean literally enlarging the physical facilities, but this option might not be economical if the expanded facilities are used only during very short peak periods. Less expensive options to speed service or otherwise expand the business's capacity include automating tasks, cross-training workers to perform multiple tasks during peak operating hours, hiring additional workers or training customers to self-serve portions of the service.

If service capacity often exceeds demand, you could try to increase capacity use during slow periods. These efforts might include educating customers about the benefits of using the service during nonpeak times (such as no wait-ing, lower rates), or using a reservation system to steer customers into nonpeak periods. Other growth alternatives such as adding new services and new service systems can also help to fill periods of low demand.

Developing or Modifying Service Delivery Systems

Customer feedback is often instrumental in discovering new ways to revamp operations to make the service system more appealing. Refining what you do can attract new customers and increase the satisfaction and patronage of existing customers.

The most fundamental consideration is: What do customers expect from the service system? Is speed, price, accuracy or friendly service most important? Or are all these attributes important to one or more valued customer groups? Is the service accessible? Could the service delivery process be more convenient or customer-friendly? Could it be faster? Which steps in the process are most error-prone, and how can these steps be modified to minimize errors?

The answers to these questions may lead to decisions to grow the business by modifying the delivery system. For example, simply extending the business's operating hours may make it more accessible to more customers. To increase the number of customers served, it may be possible to reduce the amount of required customer contact. Prearranged contracts for ser-vices provided over an extended period may reduce the need for customers to contact the business every time they desire service. Automation may enable customers to bypass human workers altogether. In some instances, it might be possible to serve customers without requiring their physical presence (service by mail or telephone), or with only limited cus-tomer exposure to the service business (drive-thru windows, home delivery). In other instances, customers might prefer performing all or part of the service themselves, so making self-service options available represents another potential growth avenue.

Development of New Services

Adding new services to the service mix may attract new customers and solidify relationships with existing customers. The business's good reputation and knowledge of the marketplace may make this growth alternative attractive.

In fact, new service development may be a virtual necessity if customers' needs evolve beyond the business's existing mix of services, or if competitors are aggressively developing appealing new services. In the financial services arena, for example, young consumers' banking needs might be satisfied with a passbook savings account and a checking account, but they might turn elsewhere when they need car loans, credit cards or IRAs.

New service development also makes sense when new services occupy underused facilities during periods of low demand. Because much of the facilities' costs are incurred regardless of usage, new services designed for slow periods can have a dramatic effect on profitability. That's why ski resorts may reinvent themselves for campers and hikers during the summer or why fast-food hamburger restaurants introduce breakfast menus.

Introducing new services is more risky for service businesses than introducing new products for manufacturers, because the service system may have to be redesigned to accommodate the new service and employees can become overwhelmed if they must deliver and promote too many services. As a result, the company's reputation is at stake with every new service introduction; customers may be exposed to poor service quality before all glitches have been remedied.

Risk can be minimized by systematizing the process of generating and screening ideas for new services, gauging customers' reactions at each stage, involving employees in the development and testing of the service, developing and reviewing service requirement standards, training employees, introducing the service during limited time periods or at a limited number of locations (at least initially) and by opting for new services that are not radically different from existing services.

Addition of New Locations

Because service businesses usually must be located near their customers and the number of customers each service facility can serve is usually limited, expansion into new geographic markets usually means building additional facilities. These may be company-owned or franchise operations. Other location options include buying existing competitors' businesses and, in some cases, opening new distribution channels other than franchises.

Company-owned locations can be more profitable than franchises and maintaining uniform standards across locations is easier to control. Such uniformity is critical to the business's reputation, so it's advisable to refine the service system and standards before opening new locations. When operations vary too much from location to location, expenses and service quality fluctuate and customers become disenchanted with the business.

The costs of company-owned expansion can be high, both in dollars and time. Expansion efforts detract from existing operations. In particular, service to existing customers can suffer. Profitability suffers if locations are placed too close to one another and they eat into one another's sales. If locations are geographically distant, physically visiting each one can be quite time consuming, but the owner may need to inspect frequently, because local managers may not have a lot at stake in the success of the operation.

Franchising is a form of licensing by which the owner (franchisor) of the service business obtains distribution through affiliated dealers (franchisees). Today there are approximately 600,000 franchise outlets in the United States including service businesses such as Hardee's (fast foods), Western Sizzlin' (restaurants), Jazzercise (fitness centers), Fantastic Sams (hair care centers) and Maaco (auto painting), to name a few.*

---

*Additional information about franchising may be obtained from the International Franchise Association, 1350 New York Avenue, NW, Suite 900, Washington, D.C. 20005

Franchising enables the company to grow much more quickly than company-owned outlets, because each franchisee typically makes a personal investment to cover all or part of the new location's start-up costs, thereby substantially reducing the founder's costs of expansion. Additional revenues are generated through sales royalties and agreements that franchisees purchase specified equipment and supplies directly from the franchisor. The rapid expansion preempts would-be competitors, and because franchisees are investing their own money, they are motivated to make the business a success.

Franchisees sometimes try to act independently and deviate from established standards, especially if promised revenues are slow to materialize. If the franchise is successful, the franchisee may be controlled with the promise of additional franchises in the future. Otherwise, controlling franchisees with the threat of legal action may be less effective than the threat of firing managers at company-owned locations.

Your Turn   *To learn more about franchising opportunities, contractual obligations, and costs/revenues associated with franchise operations, call franchise operations in your community. Ask them for the address of their parent companies. Then write to each one for additional information about their franchise operations.*

Buy your competition not only assures rapid expansion, but buying competitors eliminates them. Although more cash typically is required to pursue this growth alternative than franchising, it is usually less than building new locations from scratch. The sellers may agree to or even prefer payment over an extended period, and outside lenders and investors may be more willing to provide funds to take over businesses with proven track records.

Before acquiring a competitor, try to ascertain why the competitor's business is for sale. Talk to the competitor, employees, customers and suppliers. Inspect the premises.

Clarify precisely what is being sold—the business's land and building? Equipment, supplies, and other tangible assets? Customer information files? Trademarks? Accounts receivable? Accounts payable? Consider including a "no compete" clause in the purchase agreement, which might specify, for example, that the seller not open or work for another business in the same industry within 30 miles of the location being sold for at least 10 years.

Design your own marketing channel may be an option for some service businesses. Airlines and hotels use travel agents as intermediaries. Banks install ATMs in convenience stores. Concert promoters use retail stores as ticket outlets. Insurance companies authorize independent agents to sell insurance policies. Because the service business provides the core service, the channel members essentially perform a marketing function. Still, the image, reputation and mistakes of the intermediaries can affect the service firm. An irate passenger blames the airline for a travel agent's ticketing error, so take care when designing alternative distribution channels and selecting intermediaries.

Integration

The most risky growth alternative is integration. A service firm might integrate backward by performing services previously subcontracted or by manufacturing its own equipment and supplies. For providers of business services, forward integration would entail entering the same business as customers; for example, a telemarketing firm selling its own line of merchandise or a golf maintenance company building its own golf course. Both forward and backward integration can be risky because they often involve entering different and unfamiliar businesses that may not capitalize on the strengths of the original business. In the case of forward integration, competing directly against customers may create ill will among customers.

Backward integration offers the benefit of decreasing dependency on suppliers or improving service quality if existing suppliers don't measure up. Forward integration can help the business improve its service by becoming more sensitive to the problems its customers face.

SUMMARY

Growing the business can boost profitability, elevate morale and enhance the business's position in the marketplace, but growth brings risks. It almost always consumes additional money, time and energy that become losses if anticipated demand fails to materialize. Moreover, pursuit of growth may lead to neglect of current operations and customers. Thus, the decision to grow is not appropriate for every business or entrepreneur.

If you make the decision to grow, several alternatives are available. Not all options are as tangible or as risky as construction of new facilities. For example, the growth avenue one might travel first is the management of the business's existing financial affairs. Improved financial management can squeeze additional profits from operations and strengthen the business's ability to pursue more cash-consuming alternatives at a later date. Other growth opportunities include increasing the purchase volume and frequency among existing customers, advertising to attract new customers, expanding use of existing facilities, developing or modifying new service delivery systems, developing new services, adding new locations, and employing forward or backward integration. Many of these growth strategies are interrelated and can be pursued simultaneously.

ASK YOURSELF

▶ Have you weighed the pros and cons of growing the business? Are you willing to accept the consequences that failed efforts might bring? If the pursuit of growth is successful, are you prepared for your personal involvement in the business to change (more travel, more administrative controls, more delegation, less time spent with customers)?

▶ Before pursuing other growth options, have you tried to improve the business's existing financial performance?

▶ Have you considered the effect of growth on your key employees and managers? Do they have the skills, experience and enthusiasm needed to pursue growth? If not, do you have a plan to grow personnel before growing the business?

▶ Considering the many growth options, have you evaluated the advantages and disadvantages of each one? Which options are most appropriate for your business?

CHAPTER
FOURTEEN

MANAGING
CUSTOMER
RELATIONSHIPS

CHAPTER FOURTEEN

THE SERVICE RELATION- SHIP CHAL- LENGE

Growing a service business often entails acquiring new customers with aggressive marketing and sales efforts, offering new services that appeal to different customers or adding locations. Yet existing customers represent a tremendous growth opportunity. Attracting new customers is only the first step. Working to keep them is the second.

Building and maintaining relationships with customers to ensure that they will return is a profitable practice for any business, but it is especially appropriate in the service sector for several reasons. When relationships are strong, customer attrition is lower, so fewer resources are used trying to replace lost customers and acclimate new ones and the cost of serving customers drops. Moreover, the quality of interactions between employees and customers is enhanced, so the quality of the service is enhanced. Both employees and customers derive some added satisfaction from seeing one another. Discussions are more likely to be candid and substantial as employees and customers work together. In the process, employees learn customers' needs and preferences, and customers feel relaxed and confident enough to offer observations and suggestions. Customers come to realize that the business does have their best interests at heart. Trust develops, and purchase volume grows. When occasional, inevitable mishaps do occur, these customers are more likely to give the service business a chance to correct the situation. Finally, when ties with customers are strong, customers talk positively about the service with other people, and these other people listen and often become customers themselves.

One study of service industries reinforced the wisdom of strengthening ties with existing customers.* The study found that the typical service business loses about 20% of its customers each year. Although some attrition is unavoidable (such as when customers move away or die), if the attrition rate could be cut only five percentage points, profits would soar 25%–85%. Not only do happily

---

*Reichheld, Frederick F. and W. Earl Sasser, Jr. (1990), Zero Defections: Quality Comes to Services, *Harvard Business Review*, September–October, pp. 105–111.

retained customers remain loyal, but they also buy more and often are much less expensive to serve.

Few business executives or entrepreneurs disagree with the importance of cementing relationships with customers, although some assert that not all customers are worth retaining. Everyone believes in nurturing customer relationships. Everyone wants profitable repeat business.

Commitment to the philosophy of relationship building is one thing, but taking steps to implement a relationship-building program is quite another. Most businesses do not have comprehensive programs in place. Most service businesses:

▶ Do not budget for building customer relationships

▶ Do not have a specific manager or employee charged with the responsibility of retaining customers

▶ Do not know what percentage of last year's customers have not purchased this year (nor have they contacted lost customers to learn why they stopped buying)

▶ Have no idea how many existing customers may be dissatisfied and close to defecting

▶ Do not have specific customer retention objectives

▶ Have never calculated the lifelong value of regular customers (Domino's Pizza estimated the lifelong value of a customer at $5,000)

▶ Do not monitor purchase records for each customer (Many do not have purchase records for each customer)

▶ Reward employees for opening new accounts, but few reward employees for efforts to keep existing accounts

Your Turn   *As a service customer, consider three service businesses that you once patronized. Why don't you do business with them anymore? Did the businesses know when you severed the relationship? Have they asked you why you no longer do*

business with them? Did they try to encourage your continued loyalty? If not, what might they have done? Have they tried to get you back? Do you believe they care?

FINDING THE RIGHT MIX

As any baker knows, there is no single recipe for making a cake. An almost endless number of ingredients can be blended together in varying proportions to form an unlimited number of uniquely different cakes. Some cakes are less expensive and less time-consuming than others. Each may satisfy a different taste preference. Despite the differences, each is still a cake nonetheless.

Just as cake mixes vary, so do programs to solidify relationships with customers. There is no single best recipe that every service business should follow when designing and implementing a relationship-building program. Each program is blended with different ingredients in different proportions to satisfy different objectives. However, some ingredients are more popular than others.

Service Quality

Service quality is the most critical ingredient. Without it many of the other ingredients amount to little more than nutrition-free puffery. Customers may be sold once or twice in the absence of quality, but if the business routinely falls short of meeting customers' expectations, any hopes of a long-term relationship are doomed.

Service quality improvement means first listening to customers to understand what quality means to them and whether they believe the business's quality measures up. Quality improvement means attending to both the technical and the personal dimensions of service quality, and involving every manager, supervisor and employee in the process.

Service Differentiation

Winning the hearts and pocketbooks of customers means eliminating the competition by making the service experience so unique, so creative and so superior that competitors simply do not compare. The service may be faster, the location more convenient, the employees more friendly, the atmosphere more appealing or the value greater.

Every service business is differentiated from competitors in some way, but to eliminate the competition, the points of differentiation must be meaningful to customers, difficult for competitors to duplicate and they must be promoted.

Service Augmentation

Enhance the perceived value of the service by giving customers a little something extra, something they appreciate but don't necessarily expect. The bonus may be in the form of an interpersonal gesture, like learning and using a customer's name. It may be something tangible like a free meal, a cup of coffee, a piece of candy or an informative newsletter. It may be working harder to honor customers' unusual requests, or doing something competitors can't or won't. It may be giving a customer a gift to offset the inconvenience of a service error or as thanks for bothering to report the problem. Whatever the forms of augmentation, if they are to be effective relationship-building tools, customers must value them and recognize that they extend beyond the normal boundaries of the service.

Upcoming Innovations

Periodic innovations position the business as a leader and customers like to do business with leaders. Moreover, keeping something new on the horizon gives customers something to look forward to. Guests at DisneyWorld, for example, are shown glimpses of upcoming rides, exhibits and other attractions to entice them to return.

The innovations may be the introduction of a new service or a new service feature, a facility modernization, a contest or a big sale. In some cases, announcing the addition of a new employee or that the business is under new management may be perceived as a welcome change. In effect, promoting innovations and promising future ones subtly tells customers that today is not a good day to sever the relationship with the business.

Linking of Repeated Purchases

Link purchases in some way so that transactions are not discrete, but part of a series of purchases. For example, a consulting firm might meet with clients after the services are performed to assess client satisfaction, but also to identify remaining issues that could be resolved in a follow-up project.

Often purchases are linked together with some form of incentive or equity that customers would lose if they discontinue their patronage. Fitness and sports buffs know that committing to a long-term membership package or buying a season ticket is more economical than paying separately for each visit to the health club or buying tickets to each game separately. A movie theater might give patrons coupons good for a discount on their next visit. The discount is lost if coupons are not redeemed. McDonald's Happy Meals usually include toys that are part of a series of toys. Children feel compelled to return weekly to make sure they collect all the toys in the series. Airline passengers sign up for frequent flier programs knowing that free trips and other benefits materialize only if they continue to accumulate mileage.

Consumption Chain Marketing

Many service customers' purchases are sequential. As their needs, tastes, spending power and trust in the service business evolve, so does the mix of services they purchase. As the illustration shows, a 16-year-old consumer may launch a banking relationship with a passbook savings account and gradually progress to other bank services.

Recognizing the likely sequence of chain links enables the service firm to allocate marketing efforts more efficiently by focusing on adjacent links. The probability of selling a checking account to the 16-year-old is much greater than selling distant links such as business loans or estate planning. Service businesses that fail to develop several links of services run the risk of being unable to attract new customers at the low end of the chain, or losing customers who outgrow the business's ability to serve them at the higher end.

Consumption Chain for a Bank's Services

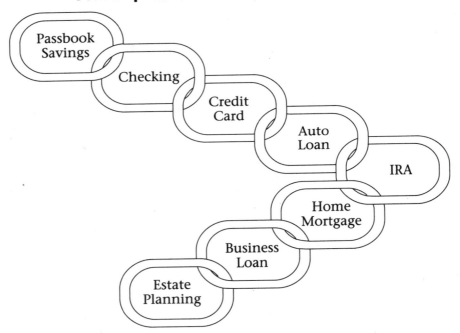

Continuity of Communications

Customers sometimes sever the relationship because they forget about the business or believe that the business has forgotten about them. In either case, it's advisable to contact customers periodically to remind them that they are valued. Such reminders are especially appropriate when the business is small and doesn't do a lot of advertising, or when the service is usually purchased infrequently anyway so that customers are likely to forget the name of the business.

Systems Friendliness

Most of us can think of examples when we've called a business only to be left stranded on hold or shunted to a voice mail maze, or we've tried checking into a hotel only to find that the hotel had lost our reservations. Emergency patients sometimes must fill out medical history and insurance forms before being allowed to see a physician.

Businesses should continuously evaluate and upgrade services and the service delivery systems to make sure the business is easy and convenient for customers to use. Ideally, customers should enjoy patronizing the business.

Service Recovery

Most service businesses have too many details in production and delivery to expect flawless operations all the time. Occasional mishaps are inevitable. Although the business should try to minimize errors, other efforts should help both the business and customers to recover from the mishaps that do occur. To illustrate: Employees may not need great interpersonal skills for routine services offered by a credit card company, because customers may go for years without ever talking to a representative. But when a customer discovers a statement error, a new set of processes are triggered, including the employee's interpersonal skills. If the credit card company is caught unprepared at such a critical moment of truth, the future of the relationship is jeopardized.

Service entrepreneurs and managers should think and plan not only in terms of delivering great routine service, but great problem-resolution service as well. Correcting the error or restoring the service is only the first step in the recovery process. Restoring the relationship may require additional steps to offset the inconvenience, anxiety or other losses incurred by customers who may perceive themselves as victims.

Unconditional Service Guarantees

Interwoven with service recovery systems are service guarantees or other pledges to honor commitments to customers. If guarantees are promoted to customers, unconditional and easy to invoke, customers are more likely to speak up when problems arise. Moreover, traditional approaches to complaint-handling might placate dissatisfied customers, but a key advantage of unconditional service guarantees is that they often prevent customers from ever becoming dissatisfied. In fact, if a guarantee's reward for lousy service is significant, some customers might actually look forward to experiencing such disservice!

Stimulation Control

Business owners often assume that defectors were dissatisfied with some aspect of the service and that they made a conscious decision to stop doing business with the service provider. In many instances, however, lost customers never were dissatisfied, and they never decided to sever the relationship. Instead, they became bored and distanced themselves from the business.

The remedy is to add excitement or variety, which is especially important when customers are routinely exposed to the service. Restaurants add new menu items or develop weekly specials. Banks replace carpet before it becomes noticeably worn. Physicians keep current magazines and other up-to-date reading materials in their reception areas. Insurance companies add new products to give agents a fresh and enthusiastic reason for contacting clients. In other service businesses, employee dress, signage, promotional materials, logos and letterheads are periodically modified or revamped.

Customers do have different thresholds of stimulation. Some customers become bored very easily, but changes can be anxiety-producing for others. To mediate the two extremes, avoid too many radical changes. Phase in change gradually, and if possible avoid phasing out the comfortable too quickly, if at all. For example, some customers may enjoy a new, automated, self-service piece of equipment, but others may prefer the option of interacting with humans who provide the service.

Affective Engineering

Affective engineering means evoking consumers' emotional responses so they feel happy in the relationship. "Feel good" advertisements that associate the business with heartwarming ideas is one way to engineer affect.

Another approach is community involvement or sponsorship of charitable causes or other events to demonstrate that the business and its owners want to give something back to the community that supports it. The community benefits, and the company gets all the free publicity that accompanies such causes and events.

Relationship Pricing

To keep them coming back, reward loyal customers with better prices. KOA Kampgrounds sells "Value Kards" to customers for a nominal price. Among other benefits, the cards entitle campers to discounts at the campgrounds. About three or four camping nights usually recoups campers' investment in the card, after which the savings accumulate. In addition to cementing relationships with customers, KOA maintains a customer database and tracks purchases for each cardholder.

Continuity or frequency programs are another twist on the relationship pricing concept. Customers at participating Blockbuster Video stores may join the Frequent Rental Club. Members receive a membership card that is punched after each rental. After nine paid rentals, the tenth rental is free—in effect, a 10% discount to reward loyal customers.

Personalization

Nobody likes to feel that they're a statistic. Learn and use customers' names, and don't act impatient when serving customers. Empower employees to deviate from scripts and rigid procedures when serving customers who have special needs or unique requests, which could mean customizing the service altogether. Opt for reservation systems rather than risk long, visible waiting lines that reinforce customer perceptions of being statistics. Assign employees the responsibility of serving customers rather than the responsibility of performing tasks. Customize the sales presentation and use highly targeted media to reach customers.

Customer Information File

Today's computer technology makes it much more cost efficient to build databases that catalogue basic customer information (names, addresses and phone numbers), as well as track customer purchases, preferences and other information. The data could identify the characteristics and preferences of high-volume or loyal customers, who could then be recognized for their patronage (for example, with thank-you notes or birthday cards). The data could be used to direct specific promotions to specific groups of customers; the results could then be analyzed and stored in the database for future efforts.

Knowing who the customers are, how they can be contacted and what their purchase histories are enables the service business to calculate the annual customer attrition rate—the percentage of last year's customers who do not purchase this year. Information gathered from follow-up surveys or informal contact with retained customers can be added to the database and used to understand why these customers are satisfied and what the business should do to continue earning their loyalty. A follow-up with former customers may reveal why they no longer do business with the company and what might be done to get them back.

Examination of the data could show that customers send up warning flags before they sever their ties with the business. They purchase in smaller quantities, are late with payment, lodge complaints that go unresolved, hesitate signing a purchase agreement or fail to return phone calls. Customer defections may coincide with changes in personnel, prices or operating policies and procedures. Understanding these signals and promptly responding to them is a critical step in curbing the number of lost customers, because it is easier to prevent customers from leaving the company than it is to get them back after they have left. Without analyzing this sort of data for many customers over a long time, subtle trends and patterns may go undetected. Computers make the analysis easier.

Reinforcement

One of the oldest and most recognized theories of human behavior is reinforcement. Behavior that is reinforced is more likely to be repeated than that which is not. In the context of serving customers and strengthening relationships with them, thanking customers is one of the most potent reinforcement tools available to service businesses.

Customers like to be thanked for their business. One study found that insurance customers were more likely to renew their policies if they received a thank you letter before receiving a renewal notice.* Another study found that jewelry store customers were more likely to purchase additional items within the next 12 months if they received a follow-up phone call thanking them for their original purchase.** Still another study found that many customers—especially older ones—appreciate being thanked during virtually any contact with employees, such as when customers ask for change.***

---

*Bergiel, Blaise J., and C. Trosclair (1985), Instrumental Learning: Its Application To Consumer Satisfaction, *Journal of Consumer Marketing*, 2(4), pp. 23–28.
**Carey, J. R., et al (1976), A Test of Positive Reinforcement of Customers, *Journal of Marketing*, 40(4), pp. 98–100.
***Martin, Charles L. (1990), The Employee/Customer Interface: An Empirical Investigation of Employee Behaviors and Customer Perceptions, *Journal of Sport Management*, 4(January), pp. 1–20.

Switching Costs

Some customers may continue their relationships with the business not because they think the company is so wonderful, but because it is perceived as too costly, too risky, too inconvenient or too something else to switch to a competitor's service. A bank customer might be dissatisfied with a checking account, but opening an account at another bank may mean making several phone calls to find the best deal, taking time away from work to open the new account, keeping the first account open while recent checks clear the bank and buying new checks to replace those already purchased. Given these switching costs, the dissatisfied bank customer may postpone the decision to sever the relationship.

It is tempting to think in terms of erecting switching costs to ensure repeat patronage, but some switching costs can have undesirable consequences. If customers feel locked into relationships, they may become uncooperative or spread unflattering comments about the business. If prospective customers recognize the switching costs before entering the relationship, the costs may discourage them from signing up. For example, mutual fund shoppers may shy away from funds with heavy sales loads.

Service entrepreneurs can provide attractive incentives to offset the negatively perceived switching costs, or they can work to reduce competitors' switching costs. For example, some banks reimburse new checking account customers for unused checks left over from former banking relationships. Long-distance telephone companies sometimes waive sign-up fees or offer discounts to lure competitors' customers. Apartment complexes sometimes provide free moving services for new tenants.

Trust

Many services are not sold. Rather, what is sold is a *promise* of a service. A mortgage company promises to service a homeowner's loan. A barber promises to cut a customer's hair as requested. An attorney promises to write a defensible contract for the client. If customers do not believe service providers will honor their promises, the relationship is doomed.

Trust is a critical element in retaining customers, one that should not be taken for granted. Service providers must earn their customers' trust by honoring their guarantees and other commitments, managing customers' expectations (keep advertising claims realistic), maintaining open channels of communication with customers so misunderstandings can be quickly identified and remedied and establishing a code of ethics for employees so they too will act in a trustworthy manner. It may takes years to build trust, but it can be destroyed in an instant.

Vulnerability

Establishing business relationships with customers is like establishing personal relationships: To make a friend, you must first be a friend. Building and nurturing the relationship may mean accepting some risk, trusting customers and giving something without any certainty of receiving anything in return. To be vulnerable may mean granting credit to customers who may not be able to pay immediately. It may mean investing the time to diagnose the customer's service needs or preparing a proposal without any assurance of winning the contract. It may mean offering an unconditional guarantee while knowing that the offer will be abused by unethical customers.

Early Beginnings

Be the first service provider to ask for the sale. Being first increases the odds of capturing the customer's attention and initiating the relationship—possibly well before the customer realizes that competitors exist. Once the relationship is launched and the customer is satisfied, competitors will look much less attractive.

The beginnings of the relationship may form when new residents move into the community and learn about the business from local welcoming services such as Welcome Wagon. In some instances, the beginnings may start with a new set of needs, such as first-time parents' needs for pediatric health care services, diaper services or day care services.

The relationship may start with the children themselves. Not only do children today have more spending power than kids of past generations, but they also exert considerable influence on parents' purchases. As far as the long-term potential of the relationship is concerned, consumers exposed to services as children are likely to be loyal customers as adults.

Employee Relations

Strengthening employee relations is an indirect, yet potent way to enhance customer relations. It is doubtful that employees can cheerfully and enthusiastically make customers happy if they are not happy themselves.

Sometimes the term internal marketing is used to stress the importance of employee relations. In this idea, employees are viewed as internal customers who consume the roles and responsibilities of their jobs. Just as it is common practice to seek out prospective external customers, it is also appropriate to take a marketing approach to find and recruit well-qualified job applicants. Just as you want to be sensitive to the needs and preferences of customers, you want to listen to the concerns of employees.

Customer Compatibility

Customer relations usually mean the relationships between customers and the business, or those between customers and front-line employees. Indeed, most customer retention efforts focus on these two areas. Another area for concern in customer retention is the relationship between customers and other customers. Customers may feel uneasy, threatened or otherwise dissatisfied if they are incompatible with other customers in their presence. Restaurant patrons may not be able to tolerate other customers who smoke, shout, have strong body odors, stare, break in line, have an untidy appearance, fail to supervise their children, use obscene gestures or profanity or tell racial jokes.

Some of these customer behaviors are more controllable than others, so it is in the service business's best interest to identify and act on the most problematic ones. Addressing these behaviors might involve directing marketing efforts to a largely homogeneous clientele (children admitted for half-price during Saturday matinees), establishing standards of customer conduct (shoes and shirt required), separating incompatible customers (smoking and nonsmoking sections) and manipulating the physical facilities (providing ample seating so incompatible customers won't have to sit near one another).

Time

Time is not a strategy or technique, but it is necessary for trust to develop, for customers to test the strength of the bond and for a relationship culture to grow in the business. Programs to build customer relationships are destined to fail if they are tried for a couple of months and then dropped if they are not immediately successful. Instead, patience and persistence are called for. The results will follow.

Always build for the long term in customer relationships. Once I watched a group of bowlers as they paid for about 20 games, more than twice the average number of games for a party their size. The attendant totaled the bill on the cash register. When one of the women in the group reached into her purse for the money, she found a coupon for a free game of bowling. After laying the coupon on the counter, she became disgruntled when the employee explained that he could not accept the coupon because he had already rung the amount on the cash register; "the coupons must be presented before the amount is tallied." In protest, the lady paid the full amount and stormed out of the bowling center—perhaps never to return.

SUMMARY

Service business growth is often thought of in terms of attracting new customers, building new locations and selling franchises. However, most service firms could realize substantial growth in profitability—from 25% to 85%—by developing and implementing a comprehensive customer retention program.

Several elements may be combined to create a unique customer retention plan. The mix includes:

- ► *Service quality.* Consistently meeting customers' expectations

- ► *Service differentiation.* Making the service unique

- ► *Service augmentation.* Enhancing value by giving the customer something extra

- ► *Upcoming innovations.* Keeping something new on the horizon to enhance value and give customers something to anticipate

- ► *Linking of repeated purchases.* Ensuring that there is no opportune time for the customer to sever the relationship

- ► *Consumption chain marketing.* Cross-selling multiple products or services in a logical sequence based on customer needs

- ► *Continuity of communications.* Avoiding extended periods of time during which the customer is not contacted or exposed to the company's advertising

- ► *Systems friendliness.* Ensuring that the business is convenient for customers to contact and patronize

▶ *Service recovery.* Correcting mistakes when they occur and offsetting customers' inconvenience or other negative consequences caused by the mishaps

▶ *Unconditional service guarantees.* Honoring commitments to customers without excuses or hurdles

▶ *Stimulation control.* Interjecting the optimum amount of variety or excitement into the service, service delivery, or business atmosphere to keep the customer from becoming bored or anxious

▶ *Affective engineering.* Evoking consumers' emotional responses, often by association

▶ *Relationship pricing.* Rewarding loyal customers with better prices

▶ *Personalization.* Treating each customer as a unique individual, or customizing the service

▶ *Customer Information File.* Tracking purchase behavior and other relevant information for each customer

▶ *Reinforcement.* Encouraging customers to repeat desirable behaviors (Thank You!)

▶ *Switching costs.* Absorbing some of customers' monetary or nonmonetary expenses when shifting patronage from one company to another

▶ *Trust.* Ensuring that customers know the business will stand behind its service and honor its commitments

▶ *Vulnerability.* Taking a risk by giving the customer or prospective customer something of value without requiring a reciprocal commitment

▶ *Early beginnings.* Cultivating relationships with new consumers, new residents to the community and customers who have new needs

▶ *Employee relations.* Serving those who serve customers

► *Customer compatibility.* Fostering desirable customer-to-customer behaviors while minimizing undesirable ones

► *Time.* Practicing patience and persistence in efforts to solidify customer relationships

ASK YOURSELF

► Have you ever felt like a stranger in a service business the first time you visited the business? What did the service workers do (or what might they have done) to make you feel welcome and appreciated?

► Have you ever felt like a stranger in a service business you have frequently patronized? What did the business do to contribute to these feelings? What will you do in your service business to prevent your loyal customers from having similar experiences?

► In what ways is the process of building and maintaining business relationships with customers similar to building and maintaining personal relationships with your friends and family? How is it different?

► Although it is in your best interest to establish long-term relationships with customers, have you considered how customers might benefit from such long-term relationships? Viewing the relationship from their vantage point will increase the chances of assembling an effective relationship-building program.

SERVICE LEADERSHIP: PUTTING IT ALL TOGETHER

CHAPTER FIFTEEN

WHAT IS LEADER- SHIP?

Being the company founder or the designated boss is not the same as being a leader. Although one may have the formal authority to make decisions and give orders, there is no guarantee that workers will rally behind the decisions or commit themselves to the directives. As former President Dwight D. Eisenhower once said: You do not lead by hitting people over the head—that's assault, not leadership.

Leadership is the ability to motivate service personnel to pursue the company vision and objectives enthusiastically. It involves the realization that the business cannot succeed by the sole efforts of the individual entrepreneur or manager. For the service business to prosper, both management and workers must pull in the same direction. To be an effective service leader, one must be a visionary, a pathfinder and a tightrope artist.

Be a Visionary

As a visionary, the service leader must have a strong sense of what the business is, why it exists, where it is going and how it will get there. The enthusiasm of the vision must be contagious and its pursuit perceived as worthwhile. The vision must be simple enough to be easily communicated to and remembered by every employee. When employees hear the vision—and they should hear it often—the relevance to their individual jobs should be apparent. That is, the vision should link employees in a common purpose, showing them how their job performance affects the business, other employees and customers.

The vision should be packaged in the form of a vision statement, sometimes called a mission statement, statement of purpose, business philosophy or similar term. The vision statement should include references to customers, service, technology, employees and the future. When you write your vision statement, think about the following questions.

► *Customers:* Who are our customers? How valuable are they to our success?

► *Service:* What services do we provide? What do these services have in common? How committed are we to service quality?

► *Technology:* How do we serve customers? How do we create value for our customers?

► *Employees:* What role does personnel play in our success? What are the characteristics of successful employees? How committed are we to employee development?

► *Future:* Where is the company going? How is it evolving in terms of markets served, services offered, size and profitability?

In addition to these fundamentals, the vision also might comment on the competition (do we want to be bigger and better?), investors (how will they be satisfied?), community involvement (what is our role as a business citizen?), creativity (are we innovators?), growth (how much, how fast, in what direction?), performance (profitability?) and ethics (do we subscribe to the Golden Rule?).

The British Airways Mission

To be the best and most successful company in the airline business.

Our Goals

► *Safe and Secure*: To be a safe and secure airline.

► *Financially Strong:* To deliver a strong and consistent financial performance.

► *Global Leader:* To secure a leading share of air travel business worldwide with a significant presence in all major geographic markets.

► *Service and Value:* To provide overall superior service and good value for money in every market segment in which we compete.

► *Customer Driven:* To excel in anticipating and quickly responding to customer needs and competitor activity.

► *Good Employer:* To sustain a working environment that attracts, retains and develops committed employees who share in the success of the company.

► *Good Neighbour:* To be a good neighbour, concerned for the community and the environment.

To achieve these goals, we must:

► Deliver friendly, professional service consistently through well-trained and motivated employees.

► Search continuously for improvements through innovation and the use of technology.

► Employ planning and decision-making processes that provide clear direction and sense of purpose.

► Foster a leadership style throughout the organisation which encourages respect for individuals, teamwork and close identification with customers.

► Strive constantly to achieve agreed standards of quality at competitive cost levels.

Be a Pathfinder

As a pathfinder or planner, the service leader must chart a course of action that will transform the promise or potential of the vision statement into reality. Involving employees in the planning process is not only likely to lead to a better plan, but employee participation also increases the likelihood that workers will be committed to the plan.

Planning to transform the vision statement into reality involves several steps, beginning with a realistic assessment of the business's situation. Consider the business's strengths, weaknesses, opportunities, modes of operation and customers served.

► What are the underlying trends and other factors that shape the demand for the service?

► What is the service? How is it visualized?

► How heterogeneous is the service? To what extent is the service customized? How is unwanted heterogeneity minimized?

► What is the optimum level of demand given existing supply? How is the timing of supply and demand managed to avoid the undesirable consequences of excesses of either?

► How do customers evaluate the service? What is the nature and quality of interactions between front-line employees and customers?

► Who are the competitors? Where are they? What is their reputation? Do they compete heavily on price?

► How is the service delivered, as shown by the service blueprint? What are the strengths and weaknesses of the system?

► What form of organization does the business employ? Is it effective?

► What are the business's standards and controls for each of the 10 components of service quality?

► What do customers expect? How do customers rate the company's service quality? Are customers' perceptions routinely and systematically sought?

► What is done to attract, screen, orient, train, motivate and supervise employees?

► How much is charged for service? How are prices determined?

► Is there sufficient untapped demand to justify a growth strategy? Would operations suffer if growth were pursued at this time? Is the business financially fit to grow?

► What are the company's past experiences with growth? Which growth options have been successful and which have been unsuccessful? Why?

► What is the nature and quality of existing relationships with customers? How valuable is customer retention to the business? What does the business do to cement relationships with customers? Which relationship strategies are the most effective?

Specification of goals and objectives may then stem from the situation analysis. In what areas are improvements needed and by how much? Next, strategies and tactics may be formulated to help the business reach those objectives.

Be a Tightrope Artist

In developing the service vision and formulating action plans to make it happen, the service leader must consider several options that can seem contradictory. Continuously faced with these sorts of decisions and having to balance one consideration against another, the plight of the service leader is not unlike that of a circus performer walking a tightrope. Being a leader means facing these issues and making tough decisions. Some of these balancing acts include:

► Standardizing the service to control costs and ensure uniformity, or customizing the service to cater to individual tastes

► Manipulating demand to meet supply, or manipulating supply to meet demand

► Establishing tight controls and detailed policies to prevent employees from failing, or empowering employees to use their own judgment and learn from their occasional mistakes

► Helping customers to provide the service themselves, or convincing them that they should let the business do it for them

► Encouraging employees to establish rapport and nurture customer relationships, or discouraging them from spending an excessive amount of time serving customers

- Cooperating with competitors for the benefit of the industry, or aggressively competing to gain a strategic advantage

- Establishing prices on the basis of short-term variable costs, or using longer-term total costs as a basis for pricing

- Making the service system as efficient as possible to control costs, or personalizing the system to strengthen customer relationships

- Encouraging teamwork, or holding individuals accountable for performance

- Decentralizing business functions to promote marketplace responsiveness and flexibility, or centralizing functions to maintain control

- Encouraging customers and employees to accept changes they may not like, or making popular decisions that may not be in the best interest of the business

- Attending to the day-to-day details of service, or planning for the future

- Competing on the basis of price, or competing on the basis of service quality

- Lowering the thermostat for customers who complain the facility is too warm, for example, or raising it for those who complain it is too cold

- Being responsive to the demands and expectations of customers, or those of employees, investors, and other constituencies

- Guaranteeing customer satisfaction unconditionally, or protecting the business from a few fraudulent customers

- Finding workers to fit the requirements of the job, or adjusting job requirements to fit the qualifications and needs of workers

► Developing skills and preparing personnel for future opportunities, or exploiting current opportunities with workers' existing competencies

► Performing the service yourself, or delegating responsibilities to less experienced workers

► Growing the service business, or fine-tuning the existing business

► Investing resources to attract new customers, or investing to retain existing ones

► Attracting new customers who are likely to be incompatible with existing customers, or curbing growth to avoid customer incompatibility

► Keeping the service fresh and exciting to prevent customer boredom, or maintaining the status quo to prevent customer anxiety

SUMMARY

Service leadership is the ability to motivate service personnel to pursue the company vision and objectives enthusiastically. Leadership is relevant to any organization, but the importance of interpersonal relationships of most service businesses magnifies the value of effective leadership. To be a service leader, one must be a visionary, a pathfinder and a tightrope artist.

In the visionary role, the leader provides direction for the business and inspires employees to work together for a common purpose. As a pathfinder, the leader involves employees to develop a plan to fulfill the vision. As a tightrope artist, the leader balances competing considerations to make difficult decisions.

ASK YOURSELF

► Do you have what it takes to be a service leader? Do you have a vision for your service business? Do you have a plan? Are you willing to make the tough decisions?

► What do you intend to do to enhance your leadership skills? How will you cultivate employees for leadership roles?

► Many of the decision choices the tightrope artist faces may appear to be contradictory and mutually exclusive, but are they necessarily so? For example, must service providers choose between standardizing the service and customizing the service, or is it possible to do both?

ABOUT THE AUTHOR

After earning a Ph.D. in marketing from Texas A&M University (1986), Charles L. Martin joined the faculty at Wichita State University, where he is currently an Associate Professor. At WSU, Dr. Martin's primary teaching duties involve courses in marketing management and services marketing. Dr. Martin has pioneered two courses at WSU focusing upon the marketing challenges faced by service organizations. His interest in service organizations has also translated into an ongoing research program examining the processes service businesses utilize to cement relationships with their customers. To date, Dr. Martin has published 9 books, including *Your New Business: A Personal Plan For Success,* Crisp Publications, and more than 170 articles for both trade and academic audiences. In addition, he is currently serving as editor of *The Journal of Services Marketing.*